by Andrea M. Thompson

The author has recreated events, locales and conversations from her memories of them. In order to maintain their anonymity in some instances, she has changed the names of individuals and places. She may have also changed some identifying characteristics and details such as physical properties, occupations and places of residence.

Most Scriptures are derived from the public domain version of the King James Version of *The Holy Bible*. Isaiah 54:11-17 has been taken from *THE MESSAGE*. Copyright © 1993, 1994, 1995, 1996, 2000, 2001, 2002. Used by permission of NavPress Publishing Group. Quotations have been sourced and attributed to the best of the author's knowledge.

Quantity Sales Ordering Information: Special discounts are available on quantity purchases by corporations, associations, and others. For details, contact the author at this address:

c/o A.M. Thompson Enterprises, LLC

1440 W. Taylor Street #1725

Chicago, IL 60607

ISBN: 978-0-578-73606-8

Library of Congress Control Number: 2021912751

Editor & Internal Book Graphic Designer: Renée Purdie

Book Cover Designer: Rachael Turner

Cover Photograph of Author: Carl Ankrum

Photographer for the "Valley Shots": Clarence Cooper, Jr.

Double Dutch Photo of Author: Matt Difanis

# Advance Book Reviews

## (Why YOU should read this book!)

*Extremely moving. It's refreshing to experience Andrea's vulnerability as so colorfully depicted in her personal journey towards "Becoming."*

*Scott L. Steward*
*Founder, Genius Lab, Inc.*

*Andrea read me an excerpt from the book about a defining moment in her life: when she met First Lady Michelle Obama. Hearing Andrea's story in her own words was very poignant. She is such an engaging narrator and I am personally excited to listen to the audiobook when she releases it! Something striking about Andrea is how she is always thinking about how she can spread knowledge and resources to others who have experienced struggles similar to her own.*

*Sasha Solov*
*Coach*
*LIFT Chicago*

*From the very first chapter, I knew that this book was absolutely amazing! The book starts off with Audacious Altitude and elevates as it lifts the spirits of its readers. I was fortunate to be among the first few to hear Andrea read the book in her words with her own voice and my first thought was ... "Well done Queen! From Meeting Michelle Obama to reaching the shores of South Africa, this book, which really is a movement, is set to soar."*
*Hope Miles*
*Founder, Lady Hope Exclusives*

# Dedication

To My Son Aric Jeremiah,

You deserve all the words and are my world.
You are the closest reflection of God's love for me.

The work is for you and speaks to you.

Your name means to exalt.

You've seen me fight the good fight
for your future and our legacy.

You're strong too.
You are music.
You are art.
You are my heart.

God's got us and your future is blessed
by the prayers I've made and continue
to make on your behalf.

**Dear God,**

**I WAS becoming.**
**I AM becoming.**
**I WILL overcome.**

I thank you for keeping me in the process towards the progress. Oh Lord, that you would give me the tools to not just go but to go the distance ... to endure and to do it all with grit and grace.

> **"The moment anyone tries to demean or degrade you in any way, you have to know how great you are. Nobody would bother to beat you down if you were not a threat."**
>
> **—Cicely Tyson**

To the business women with stories I could relate to like Forever FLOTUS Michelle Obama, Rev. Dr. Jeanne Porter King, States Attorney Kim Foxx, Marki Lemons-Ryhal, Cheryle Robinson Jackson and soooo many others.

To the female music artists of my time whose life and music made me feel the most: Mary J. Blige, Fantasia and Jennifer Hudson.

Whether the connection is that we lost brothers to violence, we grew up in the church, we lived in the projects or that we suffered childhood trauma or heartbreak, there is also another common thread of OVERCOMING. In spite of adversity, we became even better. We were in different states and forms, yet, under pressure, a diamond was produced while still serving, giving, nurturing, defending, and advocating for ourselves, our families and our communities. Thank you for showing me that we can be relentless to resolve through any storm because we are fortified in the Word and compelled to withstand the challenges on the journey.

**We are wine, fire,**
**music, food, water.**
**We are ESSENTIAL.**

**Editor's Note:** Andrea left a voice message saying, "I have this picture of me and Viola Davis." I continued on with my next notes. A little bit later, my head tilted sideways and what she said HIT me. I was like, "Wait! VIOLA FRICKING DAVIS???!" So, yeah, apparently Andrea was taking a break from the planning of her second POWBIZ conference on the Magnificent Mile in Chicago and went downstairs onto Michigan Avenue and happened to meet her. She had been feeling a bit discouraged. Well, what a way to refill your motivation tank! In Andrea's words, "Viola is the story of *The Audacity of Overcoming*! And she could direct the shit out of my movie with Ava DuVernay." This impromptu meeting was akin to the first time I was in Chicago working with Andrea on this book and we went across the street for breakfast and CNN showed up—and that was the day after I landed! When you're destined for greatness, great things happen!

# Foreword

I will never forget the first time I met THE Andrea Thompson who was then a brash and brazen freshman at Dillard University in the Fall of 2002. She walked into my Jubilee Scholars orientation class with all her southside of Chicago bravado and unceremoniously asked what she had to do and who she had to speak with to get transferred out of my class! In the span of that one class period, as I laid out my purpose as a Faculty Fellow and the rules of my class, she uttered repeatedly, "I gotta get outta here," and "She is trippin'" over and over again.

Now, other people might have taken offense to being prejudged and challenged by someone they had been charged to guide and to teach, but I saw the brash and brazen eighteen-year-old Andrea as bold and spirited and filled with great potential. I knew two things from that first meeting: (1) she wasn't going to be transferred out of my class, and (2) it was going to take a lot of work and effort on my part to break through the walls that this young woman had spent her whole lifetime building so that I could do what my job description dictated ... and more.

You see, it was my job to teach her to navigate the complex labyrinth of college life at Dillard University. It was my duty as a Black woman who had stumbled unaided through that same labyrinth just one decade prior to guide her so she learned to channel that raging fire in her spirit so it would forever drive and warm her, not consume her. I had to find a way to set that potential in motion so that its momentum would knock down anything that dared get in her way, and I only had two semesters to do it.

I saw in young Andrea not the tough girl that she was projecting for her classmates, but a little girl who was afraid. I saw fear spewing from her mouth that first night: fear of not knowing who she was in this new and foreign environment called "college." In Chicago, she was the tough girl, the fighter, and the dependable, overprotective big sister. This new place, as much as it represented freedom and opportunity, was filled with people who knew nothing of that girl and all that she'd had to overcome to get to the very seat that she sat in while in my class. She was fighting every day to overcome whatever negativity a girl from the southside of Chicago carried on her back and in her spirit on her way to becoming THE Andrea Thompson: college graduate, single mother, entrepreneur, influencer, mover, shaker, and change agent.

None of us knew it at the time, but Andrea and her classmates would eventually become what the university now calls "The Katrina Class of 2006" because that infamous storm of all storms hit the city of New Orleans in August of 2005, just as their senior year began. Its devastation of Dillard University's campus piled more obstacles atop the mountain that a twenty-one-year-old girl from the southside of Chicago already had to overcome to gain the honor of walking The Avenue of the Oaks on Graduation Day 2006. She had multiple jobs, a killer course load, awkward accommodations in a hotel-turned-makeshift-dormitory, and a never-ending stream of problems back home with which to contend.

From all true accounts and my own imaginings, this could have been her breaking point. She'd come through so much in four short years: a lack of financial and moral support from family and friends, her own fears and misgivings, unyielding professors in difficult courses, and now one of history's most ferocious natural disasters had destroyed her school and the city that had become her second home. This was certainly a moment in time that was meant to determine who Andrea Thompson would become. Through it all, she kept fighting, kept OVERCOMING, until she did walk that avenue under those majestic oaks in the Spring of 2006, on time and in fine fashion. And I was there to witness it, just as I'd promised her and her classmates that I would be. The joy on the face of that twenty-two-year-old woman's face as she stopped traffic and jumped out of her car to meet me as I walked toward the gates of campus for her big day was a complete 180-degree turn from the disgruntled, angry face of the eighteen-year-old that I'd met in my Jubilee Scholars orientation class just four years prior. She had persisted. She had persevered. She had OVERCOME, and this Mama Bird was so proud of Andrea the Phoenix who had risen from the ashes of so many fires that were supposed to consume and destroy her. To paraphrase one of my favorite quotes, "She'd survived because the fire inside of her burned brighter than the fire(s) around her." As car horns blared and impatient people yelled all around us, we hugged tightly and let the tears of joy flow freely for what had been, what now was, and what was yet to be.

Years later, Andrea would become enthralled with another girl from the southside of Chicago: our Forever FLOTUS, THE Michelle Obama. Andrea's lifelong drive to become a lawyer and to take that knowledge back to uplift her community was all the more fueled by what she learned about Mrs. Obama as she watched the Obamas make their historic ascent from community activism to the White House. It continued to fuel Andrea's drive to work within her community, particularly to get the Obamas into the White House in 2008, even after experiencing disappointments with getting funding to attend the prestigious law schools into which she had been accepted. Although it was not immediately clear, Andrea's trajectory and her path to changing the world was changing. Her desire to BECOME a lawyer would not come to fruition in the expected timeframe but, once again, she would have to OVERCOME in order to shift her drive toward new goals and a new purpose.

This shift has sometimes led Andrea to dwell upon what makes her different from Michelle Obama, as if the process of the latter's BECOMING did not include her OVERCOMING many things as well. My view from the outside looking in leads me to disagree. There are many more similarities than differences between the two. First of all, they share a great love for their southside of Chicago roots which keeps them anchored and "real" in a world that now sees them as different from the neighborhoods that first nurtured and embraced them. They both knew that in order to BECOME, they had to leave home and OVERCOME the world's doubts of what young Black girls from the southside of Chicago could do, what they could become, and what they deserved. No matter how tough, smart, determined, or hardworking they were, the same cruel world had chewed up and spit out others just like them, from the same place they're from. Who knows what characterizes the different outcomes as there are many factors, but the one that certainly sets Andrea apart is her abiding connection to God.

While THE Andrea Thompson loves and is absolutely inspired by the story of THE Michelle Obama, and still examines her own greatness through the lens of what she finds great in her icon, I see that she IS Michelle Obama. Before I knew that there was a Michelle Obama, I knew a determined, intelligent young woman named Andrea Thompson from the southside of Chicago. It has been my honor and my pleasure to watch her grow and evolve, and to conquer obstacles time and time again. And, after having the audacity to OVERCOME, she is finally giving herself permission to BECOME all that I saw in that bold and spirited eighteen-year-old so long ago. This bold book is the culmination of all that I saw in her.

*Stephanie C. Armelin, Faculty Fellow 2002-2003*

*Dillard University*

*New Orleans, Louisiana*

## A Note from Andrea

I was still a freshman and I saw the seniors lined up to take pictures. I stood in line like I was supposed to be there. I figured someone would find out I was just a freshman, but I needed to put on that cap and gown and I needed an image of it to see that it was possible for me! I nervously filled out the paper thinking someone would ask for my senior ID, but I managed to make it through and take my freshman pre-graduation pic. My roommate Aina just laughed at me like, "That's that 'Chicago crazy'!" as we jokingly called it when I did something daring.

I didn't think they would send my graduation picture proof, but they did! When I got it, I put it on my goal board. (I don't think I had heard of vision boards yet.) The following week, I was called into my advisor's office and she said, "Andrea, you just insist on ruffling these people's feathers. Can you tell me why there is a picture of you with the graduating class and you're just making it out of freshman year?" Confidently I said, "I needed to see it to know that I could! I wasn't trying to be photographed with the senior class; I just needed the proof!" By the proof, I meant the picture proof and the proof of confirmation in seeing myself in a cap and grown. She just looked at me and said, "OK, I'll tell the people. You just something else." I said, "Thank you for making my strange actions understandable to your fellow faculty." Ms. A definitely earned her checks working with me!

Three years later, I took the real deal photo! I was tired and had been through a lot, but I had made it! What meant the world to me though was I had my little sisters by my side. I'd worked overtime at a parking garage to pay the last $2,000 of the tuition. I had carried an outstanding balance since freshman year. Every year, financial aid talked to me about resolving my balance or going home, and each year somebody would write a letter of support for me to stay in school. God made a way for me to pay it in full so that I could walk across the stage. It wasn't only about doing it for me, but it was also about doing it so others could see that it was possible.

# Editor's Preface

I debated about including an Editor's preface as I want you to get to the core of the book, but I wrote it because I am truly passionate about this project. It started out as a book and became a movement. It was unconventional from the beginning, and almost every part of it did not conform to the usual, rather orderly way I prefer the editing process to go. However, this is just not the kind of book you can put in a (figurative) box.

*The Audacity of Overcoming* is a one-of-a-kind book and was also a one-of-a-kind editing experience. Editors are midwives. Sometimes we see the idea of books before or as they are conceived. Sometimes we are there to simply catch the baby as it comes out, almost fully formed. It depends on the writer and the circumstances.

I was blessed enough to see this book in Andrea when it was a spark in her beautiful eyes. I heard it when she spoke on Periscope. I saw it in her content. I believed it when I saw her smile that million dollar smile.

When I saw the first words in a document, I was super excited to see it coming into fruition, but I always knew it would. It's been a long and winding road as Andrea will affirm, not because Andrea isn't an amazing writer, not because we both didn't have the desire to birth it, but because it is such a weighty book. Even with that weight though, it frees you at the same time that it assigns you some of the purpose and vision that Andrea has been mantled with.

In this book, you can hear some of the voices of the women who came before her as Andrea always—and I do mean always—gives credit where it's due. You can feel the waves of the ocean under the ships as our people were taken from our homeland and when she flies back to South Africa, you can see them smiling and saying, "We are home." You can feel the gravity and oratorial weight of Frederick Douglass when she discusses law school, hospitals, courtrooms and the other places where the memo "justice for all" has not yet reached.

So now that you know a bit about the history of the book, let's talk about what's in it for you.

Well, for the nosy, yes, there's tea to be had (buy your box!), but because THE Ms. Andrea Thompson keeps it classy, it's tea that is meant to provide a lesson and a blueprint for avoiding harm to yourself and your family.

For the entrepreneurs, there are numerous lessons about resiliency and pivoting during extremely challenging situations. It also speaks to repositioning.

For women, there's advice about real love and what it really looks and feels like, love that begins with loving yourself.

For men, there's a real heart-to-heart look at how your interactions with us can make or break us. We love you and we want you to love us. This book shares a glimpse into the best forms of that love.

For WORLD CHANGERS, you will start to believe you can do ANYTHING you set your mind to. After all, Andrea managed to meet FOREVER FLOTUS Michelle Obama TWICE!

For parents, you will see yourself in this book, how you want the best for your children and how you will push yourself harder than you ever have to give your child what he or she needs.

I told Andrea early on that every Editor wants at least one Harry Potter book. There's no doubt in my mind this is one of mine. Andrea is a super star and this book is her time to SHINE!

*Renée Purdie*

*CEO, Rising Star Entrepreneurial Enterprises, LLC*

# Contents

# Introduction

**"I write about what breaks my heart.**

**What I don't understand.**

**And what I wish I could change."**

**—Terry McMillan**

Writing this book was incredibly painful at many points in the process. I found that my most profound writing and business strategies came early in the morning before the sun rose. I would spend hours in the dark in the bathroom with just one candle and when it burned down, I'd use the flashlight on my phone. I couldn't figure out why my writing seemed to flow better when I wrote by hand in the dark in the bathroom. I was explaining this phenomenon to my cousin and she reminded me that I used to do that as a kid. I'd forgotten all about it.

**"We write because we believe the human spirit cannot be tamed and should not be trained."**

**—Nikki Giovanni**

My birthday was in just a few weeks and whatever I thought I was going to do to celebrate it was now redirected causing me to pivot because the majority of the country was experiencing a lockdown! I thought about The Resurrection just a month before my birthday. I felt like I was not only going through a shift, a next level leveling up, but an incredibly painful stretching. My personal life was being refigured while my business life was too. The closer I got to the goal and God's plan for my destiny, the cleverer the enemy became. It was in isolation and social distancing that I drew closer to God and heard His voice affirm what I knew to be true, yet I still questioned, "Why me though Lord?" I desperately wanted to know the purpose behind the pain and the lesson in the blessing.

Why is it that the person who is to break generational curses is typically the black sheep? The main reason is people fear what they can't understand and attempt to break down what speaks to their insecurities. I had to learn not to take it personally because often the hate they give you really has nothing to do with you. Your shine forces them to see the dim spots in their own light. Stay on high beam! Don't you dare adjust your shine or dim it to your own demise.

**"As we let our own light shine,**
**we unconsciously give other**
**people permission to do the same.**
**—Marianne Williamson**

This isn't a sad story, although there are points that might make you sad, as they surely did me. Don't feel sorrow for me. This book was written in truth "with intentional and intensive purpose" (in the words of Marianne Williamson). There is a survivor tone and despite periods of being and feeling victimized, I will be vindicated (that's the next book). I am not a victim of any circumstances for I have and will continue to be resolute in my faith that God will use the valley too as I press toward the victory. There is a process to the progress.

The Audacity of Overcoming playlist is full of inspirational music by some of the most talented artists. Looking back, it seems like I had a song to go with the most meaningful moments that made them feel "real" yet real survivable still. The rough parts in the road prepared me to endure on the journey. When I needed to be reminded of this the most, I listened to "Necessary" by Fantasia. In moments of the most uncertainty, I remembered Yolanda Adams singing "In the Midst of It All" and one of my favorites "The Prayer." My praise and overcoming playlist made me "feel like going on" Five Heartbeats style. Follow the movement on the GITUP Facebook page.

Why am I telling all my business and why should you care? I don't want y'all to think I am on some *Queen Sugar* Nova trip writing this book, but like Ava DuVernay I wanted to write the truth in love, a script that shows the sides of growth, healing and forgiveness too. This is no shame and no "woe is me" story. The heart of this book is a keeping it real story of consistently overcoming with a relentless spirit that could only have come from a divine covering. There was something in me—beyond me—that kept me pushing, looking for light in the darkest places. It wasn't because I was super strong because as strong as I was, I had been broken, and I had to work very hard to rebuild.

I'd given up on trying to be superwoman. I wasn't a robot. My heart was made of flesh even though over time I felt like it was growing more like stone. I wanted to love but everything that showed me love also showed me pain. I equated the two as close relatives, even conjoined twins, as if one couldn't exist without the other. So this is a story about heartbreak, huh? Well a little bit, but not exclusively.

So am I going to take you on a rollercoaster ride? Well, kinda. Let's call it a trip, a flight, with critical phases on the way to our destination. See, with so many strong themes and powerful stories, it's hard to put this book in a box (But we did! #shamelessplug to The INBox! Go cop that!)

GITUP covers heartbreak, family issues, workplace wars and business battles too. So it's all over the place? Well, isn't life sometimes? It's at the times when it seems that the puzzle isn't coming together that God positions us perfectly to pull the pieces together so intricately in a way that creates a beautiful picture with far more depth than we could ever create without the presence of the Master. As the saying goes, it takes a master to make a masterpiece. This book is purposed to inspire, empower and give you fireproof faith, faith that will fortify you in an electrifying way because God truly is the Ultimate Plug, especially in a force by fire state.

We are ultimately talking about the journey to finding and falling in love with YOURSELF and living your best life on God's terms! It's a very real story of overcoming and becoming, a story about the relentless pursuit to carve out an untraditional path to success when the blueprint is abridged or nonexistent.

Don't follow the path chartered for you, but go your own way. The mandate to create a path and leave a trail is often applicable, yet that is not to say you don't have to be aware of points where it is best not to reinvent the wheel. This is when mentors and wise counsel come in. Yet, people can only tell you based on their experiences, environment and perspective. This can be instructive, but then there are those real dark times—I mean times when you feel like you might not make it. Those are the times when you have to desperately connect and closely too. It is connecting to the source, the creator, the Alpha and the Omega that will give you strength to make it through. When they throw stones, you will build. When they give you lemons, you will make a sweet lemon tea. This can be your construction phase as you bring products and services to the marketplace. Check out The Audaci-Tea®!

I worked as a manager in the transportation industry for years. I traveled back and forth for scholarships, work and service trips. I worked as a train attendant, a flight attendant, and a manager for five different car rental companies. So much of my experiences were shaped while enroute somewhere, whether it was by road, train, boat, or my favorite, by plane. If I had a song for it, it'd be "Bag Lady"—shout out to Erykah Badu who is a whole vibe ("you gon' miss yo' bus", plane in my case). I seemed to always be running through airports looking for gates. The port was symbolic in more ways than one. I was often going somewhere to do something (that somebody said I couldn't). I felt it was to advance myself and prove them wrong, but I didn't learn until later that my real purpose in being stretched and positioned was far greater than proving any naysayer wrong.

God spoke to me most in transit. I heard from Him the most during the elevation process and in the darkest of spaces. Crisis is the perfect opportunity for a blessing to show up more powerfully than ever if we just endure. That is the audacity of overcoming.

**Rest when you need to be restored.**

**Recharge when you're running low.**

**But <u>always</u> remain resilient!**

# Chapter 1

## Purpose Rooted In Pain

Before I formed thee in the belly I knew thee; and before thou camest forth out of the womb I sanctified thee, and I ordained thee a prophet unto the nations.
JEREMIAH 1:5

My grammar school graduation had just passed and that summer I wrote about something so painful to me that when I later read the words, I stopped writing about real life experiences. I started writing about what I dreamed of seeing in my mind and in my notepad. The world was too cold for a girl not to have a fairy tale to live in, even if it only existed in my mind. I still work best in a dark place, but light definitely illuminates brighter in a dark place. That seemed to remind me that like many examples of how God's people experienced their journeys, the most progress happens in the darkest places and during the darkest times. Ironically, pain made me stop writing as a kid and pain made me return to writing about my life again.

## Southern Hospitality

One of my earliest travel experiences was going down south to Arkansas with my Grandma. Often times we drove, but this particular time we got to take the plane there. Even as a kid, I loved the quiet of the south—sitting on the porch drinking sweet tea listening to the old folks talk about the good old days. I admired their Southern sayings delivered with a Southern drawl. I even noticed that the stars seemed to shine brighter in the south. Sometimes I would just gaze at the sky. I was a deep little kid.

I often woke up to the smell of grits, eggs and bacon (turkey bacon after Grandma met a Muslim man that turned her from the "swine"). I could tell what kinda mood Granny was in whether she was playing Aretha Franklin's "I Say a Little Prayer," Sam Cooke's "A Change Is Gonna Come" or Mahalia Jackson's "What A Friend We Have In Jesus" kind of playlist on her DVD player. I learned so much at the proverbial and sometimes literal feet of my Granny because I spent plenty days at Granny's house. I would pretty much always wake up to the smell of grits with a little bit of brown sugar (no shade to the people that like it with a little salt).

Probably the most country of my Grandma's kinfolks was Uncle Joe. Uncle Joe was 6'4", always wore overalls, lived in a shack with an outhouse with his wife Betty who had a five-inch toenail. Another notable feature was the pig pen in front of the shack. My Uncles on my Dad's side swore that pigs were the worst thing known to mankind, but Uncle Joe loved his pigs, even the one with one ear.

One day while I was trying to figure out whether the pig lost its ear to the dog or one of the cows, I saw a big turtle slowly taking a stroll across the dirt road. I was so excited to see a turtle live, up close, and in person that without considering I was putting the turtle at risk, I excitedly said, "Grandma! Grandma! A turtle!" Before I knew it, Uncle Joe was standing on the edge of the porch with the longest shotgun I had ever seen looking like, "I got you sucka." Within seconds, the turtle was no more. He dropped his head down to the dust. Uncle Joe seemed pretty excited that he had just conquered supper, while I was sad that I had been the one who had dropped a dime on Speedy.

Aunt Betty went to work on that turtle and by dinner time Granny was feeling a little adventurous. I just stared at my Granny while she was trying to convince me that it tasted just like chicken. Each time she took a bite, she said, "It's good baby. Just take a little bit." There wasn't ever gonna be enough hot sauce for the Chicago in me to be okay with eating that turtle! I was not about to partake in a meal which included a creature I just saw living its best life. It's a good thing that I didn't because when we got ready to head to the airport the next day, Granny's arm had started to swell. By the time we made it to the gate, her affliction had become so noticeable that she wasn't allowed to board. The next day I convinced her to go back to the airport and put my coat on her arm so that we could make it home. With my coat wrapped around her arm and with my arm wrapped over the coat, we were able to make it on board.

As soon as we landed, Grandma made a beeline to Michael Reese Hospital. You shoulda seen the doctor's face when she said she had eaten turtle meat. The doctor got seven interns to look at her arm. Just like that, she had become a science project. Apparently the turtle meat had made Grandma sick. Interestingly, when she called back down south, Uncle Joe and Aunt Betty were doing just fine. Looking back, this may have been my first example of how different people can have the same experience and get a different outcome. It's also important to understand that you have to be careful about what you ingest, and not just physically.

From that point on, Granny treated turtles like drugs and just said no. To this day though, when I think about Uncle Joe and the way he didn't think twice about killing that turtle, it makes me think that maybe he also had something to do with that pig's missing ear!

## Grammar School: Lessons in Self-Love

I was a girly tomboy. I danced, cheerled, played basketball and climbed trees too. I remember skipping a step on the wooden balance beams and the stump hit between my legs. It hurt so bad! I thought back to my Dad's instructions to kick a boy in his nuts if I had to get 'em off of me. I really didn't know what nuts were, but I guessed it was what they called their "pocketbook." Not only did I break down, but I cried and bled too. I didn't want to tell my Mom that I hurt myself, especially not "down there." I didn't know what she would think or if I'd be in trouble. So I did what any wise kid would do … I took a bath, towel dried off, and got the bright idea to dab a little peroxide to prevent infection. (I knew rubbing alcohol wasn't going to go well down there). I then put on what I thought back then were big band-aids that I found in the linen closet. I had seen my Mama use them for bleeding, so I did too. The bleeding stopped.

A couple weeks later, I started to bleed there again and I immediately thought, "Now, how did I hurt myself there again?" I was so confused when the big band-aid was more full than what I'd seen before when I hurt myself. I said, "Oh, if this doesn't stop I'm going to have to tell somebody that I hurt myself down there again." I hoped it would stop soon as I definitely didn't want anyone looking down there. I was mortified. Two days later, I learned that I'd started this thing called a period and it was a completely natural thing, despite it being painful and feeling like a curse. It's funny how some natural things are so foreign to us that we never really embrace them as a beautiful process but more as a painful cross or burden to bear.

I initially felt the same disdain about what I later realized was natural beauty. Actually, I was taught to feel this way. There was this dope female rapper from New York who was hot back then. She wore different color wigs and although I couldn't quite yet understand a lot of the sexual innuendos, I later understood what she meant when she talked about some of the reasons for her surgeries. Exotic and foreign were emphasized and the darker you were, the further from beautiful you were, or at least that's what dark girls with afrocentric facial features who didn't have "good hair" were often made to feel. That lesson came early on.

This topic also came up with my son. He started to take notice of hair at a very young age. My son was about two when we were at a church in Boston and he made friends with a little white girl. He gently rubbed her hair before rubbing his own and looking at me with curiosity. He said "hair" pointing at her before pointing back at me and saying again, "Hair Mommy." Even though he could not completely verbalize it, I knew that he was thinking her hair is different. I wanted him to see the obvious difference and learn to appreciate the difference while embracing his own.

During our time in Portlandia, he was about six when he told me, "Mommy, I like when you have flat hair instead of big hair. Nice and straight is how I like you to wear your hair, not really when it's nappy." I don't know what I responded, but I know that my heart sank hearing that. I loved his afro on him, but his comments made me wonder if he loved it too. He said that sometimes he wanted to cut it, but sometimes he liked it. I hadn't expected to go through this many hair issues with a boy, but there we were. The more I thought about it, I remembered that his Dad also had a journey with his hair when we were kids. I think he may have even tried to change the texture with a perm once or twice.

I started being intentional about watching movies and displaying imagery that depicted a love and appreciation for what he'd heard called "nappy hair." One weekend he went over to a relative's house while I was working a summer trolley event in Bronzeville. I was looking to meet my son so that we could enjoy the last hour of the event when we were done filming. I was looking for his little afro and had looked right past him until he said, "Mommy, I'm right here!" I looked down and his afro had been cut off. I was furious and ready to cut off the culprits who blatantly disrespected my wishes for my son. I cried right there in McDonalds.

There and then I learned that you cannot have people who don't like you and/or don't respect you around your children. If they don't like and respect you, they will also show a disregard for your wishes for your child. That's applicable across the board even when it comes to the schools where our children spend a great deal of their day. With all that said, in India Arie fashion I got it together and reminded myself that I am not my hair and neither was hair going to make or break my son ... but the unmitigated audacity of some folks!

Back in time and back to me, I would be talking or laughing and Nana would look at me over her glasses with a disapproving look that bordered on disgust. Then she'd say, "Do your nose like this," taking her index finger and thumb and pinching downward. I would do it but it made me feel like something was awfully wrong with me. One time when we were "shaping my nose" (as she called it), I just came out and said, "I think my nose shape is based on genes. My Daddy's nose is big. I don't think this is gonna work." She said, "Well, you better hope it does or you gonna have a ugly nose spread wide across your face." I turned my head 'cause I didn't want her to see what that made me feel and I couldn't hide my expression.

There and then, at the age of 12, I decided that I wanted and needed a nose job. That was only the start of me changing my image based on what society or people made me feel was or was not beautiful. It is almost painful to expose these memories to the light, but this note from my 14-year-old self when I was in eighth grade reminded me that despite the pressure to look and be something I wasn't, and never would be, even then I was learning to fall in love with myself.

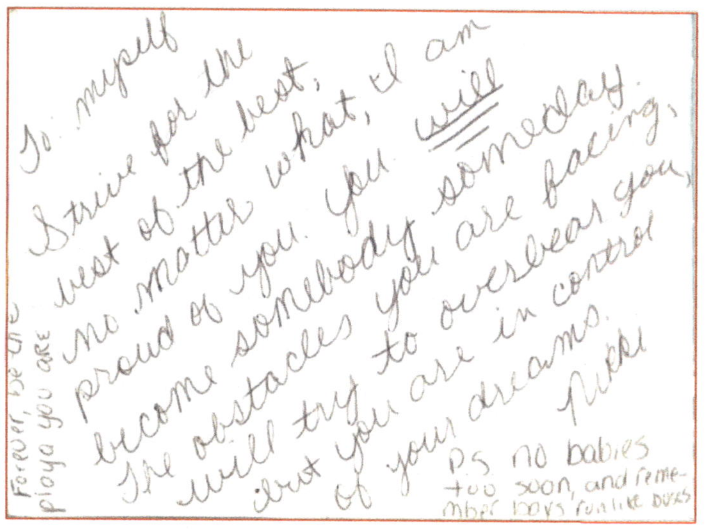

To myself

Strive for the best of the best; no matter what, I am proud of you. You will become somebody someday. The obstacles you are facing will try to overbear you, but you are in control of your dreams.

Nikki

PS no babies too soon, and remember boys run like buses

Forever, be the playa you are

## High School: Origin Story

When I got older, I started wearing the wet and wavy curl weave because it made me look mixed and that seemed to also make me more attractive. Despite getting kicked out of two schools, I made it to my senior year. I was working at UPS and taking classes at Daley Community College. The odd thing is I was getting A's in the college classes and barely making it in my classes at Kenwood. The reason for that was I was mentally done with high school. I was over the fashion shows, the fights, the playboys, the dope boys and the rich chicks too. I was ready to go to college and be great. Period. (We didn't add a t to the end back then.)

Aaron had finally convinced me to move in with him. It was the week after my Dad and I had another fight that resulted in me being put out. Instead of my normal routine of taking my bags back to Grandma's, I took all my luggage to my man's new condo adjacent to the El tracks and right next door to the store. I quickly fit into the role that I thought I was supposed to play. I made breakfast before he dropped me off at school and dinner before he came home at 7 pm to eat with me before going back out to hustle in the streets. I did our laundry on Sundays and we had date night most Saturdays.

One night I went out with my friends to a club called Nitros. He didn't like what I wore and forbade me from going out. I didn't know how serious he was until I woke up to sounds of banging like he was hammering something. I played sleep because whatever his issue was I didn't want no smoke. When I heard the door close and knew he was gone for sure I got up to check out what all the noise was. I didn't notice anything different on the walls, but when I looked down there were wood shavings on the floor. My eyes scanned from the floor to the doorknob and sure enough that's what was new. Upon further examination, I realized that this fool had installed an in and out lock. I was indeed the caged bird, but without a song. In fact, I was so flabbergasted I could barely speak! I kept thinking, "How could he leave me here locked in like an animal?!" There wasn't even a house phone, only a beeper, or maybe it was a two-way pager back then.

I was 17 and living the life of a drug dealer's wifey, not even realizing that I deserved so much better. It was as if I'd heard wind chimes as the tea kettle I'd put on started to whistle. It was as if God had given me an undeniable and absolute confirmation. "Get Out" I heard a voice say. It was over a decade before the movie came out, but just like its characters I, too, seemed to be in a trance. I snapped out of it though and grabbed a butter knife. I wasn't handy, but I started turning the ridges in the nail determined to dismantle that lock. Once I got down to the nuts and bolts, the knob fell. I stuck my finger in and triggered the lock to freedom. I grabbed a few of my things and I went back down the street to Granny's to live.

Not even three days later, Aaron called me and said, "Did you do this to me? You sent somebody to hit my spot!?" I told him I had no clue what he was talking about and swore I wouldn't do that to him. He started crying. I had never heard that kind of pain in his voice. He said, "I need you. Please come home Nikki. Please."

I felt like he was setting me up, but eventually I gave in. Just in case he thought he was going to hit me, I had my little poker in my purse. When I got upstairs and walked through the threshold of the door that had been taken off the hinges, I noticed that while the doorknob had been replaced and reinforced that didn't stop them. They managed to take the whole door off. I walked in and upon assessing the damage and the rage they must have been in, my knees got weak. We were on the top floor and the only other way out was the fire escape. I fell to the floor in tears saying, "They would have killed me!"

The intruders had cut up the mattresses, turned over the refrigerator, broken the glass table and took the backs off the TVs too! Just then I heard Aaron tell one of his boys, "They took the guns too." GUNS!!! I was afraid of guns at that time and had no idea that they were in the house with me! I thought he had installed the lock to keep me in, but maybe he guessed what was coming and was also trying to keep them out. All I could do in that moment was thank God that He told me to GET OUT because I knew for sure that those intruders would have taken me out!

It was almost prom time and I knew I didn't want to go with Aaron. Besides, he was kinda too old for prom anyway. I had every reason to be excited. I'd waited so long for this moment. I'd watched my cousins and friends' big sisters go to prom and I was ready to celebrate. This also symbolized that I was one step closer to permanently getting out of my Mama's house. That was the plan and I didn't want anything to stand in my way, not even the fine football superstar who made me temporarily forget about my abusive ex and my grammar school sweetheart from the neighborhood.

We'd met working at Coconuts music store and quickly started hanging out after work. N'eres was so patient and gentle with me. One day when I came to work with a bruise on the side of my face, he told me that his friend from school was recently killed by her abusive ex. While I was thinking about what he said, he grabbed my chin and said, "Please leave because I don't want that to happen to you." When N'eres told me about his friend, I knew it was confirmation because I had a dream about Nikki the week before. Nikki was my neighbor's best friend who worked at the convenience store by my house. I used to do her nails as a side hustle. She was cool and always smiling and giving me advice on fashion, school and sometimes boys too. I was devastated to find out that her child's father shot and killed her, leaving her only child motherless with an incarcerated father.

The confirmations kept coming. The following week I was doing homework with background music on (I never could study in complete silence) and one song came on that made me shed a tear ... "Love is Blind" by Eve. It told the story of a woman in love with an abuser and the video showed the woman's funeral at the end. At the end, it said, "For My Friend Andrea"! Through tears, I said, "Okay God, I got the message." I felt I couldn't just up and leave him, as the last time I did that he chased me down an alley until I had an asthma attack. I had to be more strategic this time, but one way or another I knew I was done for real this time.

It wasn't the next day, or the next week, but soon after I came to him with another fresh bruise and said I'd had enough. He dropped me off that night and Aaron was at the front desk of my Grandmother's building with his normal, "I'm sorry, don't leave me gifts," a bouquet of flowers and a bag with a purse or something from Breyers or the Coach store. Last time I got a Pink Panther Iceberg outfit, but this time my heart had grown ice-cold. N'eres pounced on him like a black panther. I felt bad for Aaron, but only for just one second. I was glad that somebody outside of my block brothers had put the fear of God in him, the way he did to me when he lost control.

N'eres became like a knight in shining armor after that night and he told me he wanted to always be there for me. It sounded like music in a rhythmless world. He was a man who made me feel safe and protected from even the memories of men who had hurt me badly.

## Saved in the Womb: Purpose

We started planning for prom, what colors to wear, and where he could rent size 18 shoes, but I had more important things to worry about in order to prepare. See, I had taken the one-month birth control shot and it had been taken off the market. I needed to get on something else as I didn't want to have a prom baby. I told my Mom that I had looked up that there was a Planned Parenthood on Halsted that I was gonna go to for birth control. She said so casually, "I know where that place is. That's the place I tried to abort you at." With a half-smile like it was a joke that hadn't reached the punchline, she repeated herself going further to say, "Yeah, the first time they told me you were too big and I needed more money. I came back, but in just two weeks you had grown more than double the size you were supposed to, and back then they didn't do them like they do now so they told me it was too risky. I took pills and everything, but you insisted on staying." I'd heard her say before that my Paw Paw, her father, convinced her to have me, but I hadn't known any of the details. I guess a normal person would feel sad hearing this; however, before I had a chance to sit with the weight of her words, I actually felt a little special, like God had a big plan for me that I hadn't even begun to discover.

I was the first baby girl and weighed only a couple ounces shy of 10 pounds. I was the biggest of the children, with the only above-average birth weight. There was a big destiny attached to my big delivery and whether my Mama was ready or not, I was coming into the world: bold, persistent and against all odds. God knew even then that my persistence in spite of adversity would position me to endure with promise and purpose. At the time, I didn't have a hint of the magnitude of what was in store, but I knew that God would use me in a mighty way. I remembered my Grandma's saying that "God don't make no junk." I also didn't take it for granted that He went out of His way in making and saving me. God gave me a preview, something like a glimpse of the gift, even before I could connect the intricate pieces to get a full view of the future. I knew though, even with fragmented vision, that I was purposed and one day it would all make sense.

## First Lessons In Love

One of my most memorable moments happened when I went to work in with my Grandma. This one particular client lived in the Judge Slater building (for seniors) on 43rd Street. It was nearby so we walked there. The birds had just started chirping and it was my time to chat with Grandma before she got busy with clients. One day I asked, "Is a Judge like a lawyer?" and Grandma replied, "Yeah girl, come on, I'm running late!"

I was staring out of the window wondering if a woman could be a judge when her client reached under her chair and said, "Genny, take a seat. I wanna help you with the stress on ya chest." Some of y'all may remember Ms. Cleo saying, "Call me now." Well, my Granny's client said, "Come on now." Granny didn't say anything. She just took a deep breath, put the dishrag down and sat across from Ms. Black like she was ready to lay her burdens down.

I stood up and moved towards the table watching silently in awe. Not too long after that, I could see my Grandma's face turn from curiosity to relief. Ms. Black looked at me over her glasses as if she was studying me. She said, "Let the baby sit down. It's something in her." Granny hesitated before getting up and motioning for me to have a seat. I sat there slightly confused but excited too. She stared for a while and looked surprised before saying, "Oohhh, this baby right here, my dear Lord." When she finally spoke again, she said, "Baby, you have a calling. Your destiny will be difficult in the process but it is with so much purpose. I'm gonna tell you this, there is an enemy of great danger to you, someone very, very close to you, in fact close as can be, a heavy-set, dark-skinned woman. Don't let them thwart your progress." I stood up feeling confused and not really clear about what she had said.

Grandma finished cleaning and we left. We were walking to the Cottage Grove bus to go to the next client and I was holding my Grandma's hand when suddenly I stopped walking. She looked back and asked, "What's wrong?" I looked up and said with certainty and sorrow, "Grandma, the only person I know like she described is my Mama ... She was talking about my Mama." Grandma didn't look the least bit surprised and said, "I know" before pulling my hand saying, "Nah, come on here girl fo' we miss this bus."

I thought about that for a long time. I remember later thinking, "If I can't trust my own Mama, who can I trust?" When I got older, I still wondered the same thing. I felt that she loved me, but like most love I'd experienced, it came with an unhealthy side of pain. My relationship with my Mother seemed to get better while my relationship with my Dad progressively got worse. My fly big cousin once told me he wouldn't date a woman with daddy issues because their image of men is skewed and has a bad impact on their romantic relationships. Many girls date a man like their daddy. I wanted anything but, and still got just that. I ended up dating men who were verbally or physically abusive (or both)—men that called me a B in one breath and told me they loved me in the next breath, just like my Dad did. Not only did I have daddy issues, I had mama issues too! She's said some things to me that even this book need not see.

How do you have healthy love when you see hood love that is dependent ... that can't survive without you but can't thrive with you love? If I was gonna do it, I wanted to be a power couple, not a couple struggling to keep the power on. I never really dreamed about weddings and white picket fences. In fact, I said early on I didn't want no mean husband that would lay around cheating on me and making me sad. I mean, I wanted a family and I wanted it to be with somebody I grew up with. That was the part about my parents' hood love I did want, and I wondered which boy was my boy, but I wasn't so rosy-eyed to not know that hood love was not always good love. In fact, most of the time it wasn't. I knew that the real cute chicks who stayed fly and kept their hair fresh were only checking for dudes riding real slick. They were the block "couple goals," even at times when it meant the fly girl might have to fight another chick when she caught him cheating or even worse when instead of the other chick, their man's fist met their face.

See, whether it was the dope boy, the bag boy, or the boy on the bus, they all came with a set of issues and challenges, residue I call it from their environment. Most times it was either no father in the home, or on the other hand, as in my case, a damaged presence that is damaging. My Mama had an anthem of "no romance without finance." She said, "If I had your shape, I'd never be broke." I'm pretty sure she thought that was a compliment.

I knew I wanted a man who could protect and provide for me. I didn't mind only being with him, but I wanted to feel safe because he was my man. I wanted someone to fight for me if it came down to it. I wanted to be covered by a leader and a smart man. This made me lean towards men who modeled false concepts of masculinity. Rather than fight for me, they fought with me and claimed it to be love or sought to be controlling in ways that broke me and limited my growth. In hindsight, they didn't have the strength to do the *heart* work of what fighting for me really meant. I didn't really know my worth either. I don't even know if I really loved me back then.

I knew words were powerful, but it took a while to realize the power of my thoughts and how restrictive they could be. When I got good and grown, I started to know for certain that I had a choice in what I would tolerate. Listen when I tell you I wasn't goin' for none! I almost got cold-hearted, not malicious, but numb, defensive, guarded and cynical about love. I prayed on God's promise to take my stony heart and give me a heart of flesh. I wanted to be loved properly, but first I needed to learn to love me, all of me, from my nappy hair to my not-so-narrow nose down to my big toe. I had to unlearn some of what I'd been taught and much of what I'd sought. What I had been looking for the whole time was within me.

Sometimes you are your own terrorist. Self-sabotage is real and the limiting thoughts that are rooted in a painful past based on the limiting thoughts of others can thwart your progress to success.

**The enemy will always send a terrorist alert when you are close to your destiny.**

**—Bishop T.D. Jakes**

I was determined though despite everything that was going on to go away to college and be great! I was all excited to leave for college and had saved just enough to get some of the essentials. My girl Domo worked at the Kmart, so I knew I had the hookup on toiletries and linen. To my surprise though, I went in to get the hookup and ended up coming out hooked up to handcuffs! I caught my first and only legitimate case trying to get some free stuff for school. I can write a book on being harassed and falsely arrested by the police, but this book ain't it.

So anyway, after I managed to get out of that jam on supervision rather than probation, I was ready to go away to school. Luckily, my Mama had paid my housing deposit as a graduation gift, or so I thought until I called the school and found out that gift never made it to the financial aid office. I was angry. Okay, that's an understatement. I was mad as hell! My Dad tried to console me saying I was upset because I couldn't go to a big, fancy university, but I could still go to a community college. I looked at him like he was a talking bobble head. If he thought I was going to stay in Chicago and go to a community college, he had a better chance betting on the Bulls to hit another winning spree like they did in the 90s.

Anyway, back to figuring out how I was going to make it to New Orleans when they never received my housing deposit. The dorms were full and my name was not on the list. I was mad and my Dad's community college idea didn't make the matter any better. In hindsight, his plan would have saved me a lot of Sallie Mae debt, but staying in Chicago posed too many distractions for me.

While I initially decided that I would just show up on campus without a housing assignment and figure it out, when I had calmed down a little, I talked to my Mama. She wheeled down her cooler and barbeque grill, the only one we had left since the other one had been stolen off the porch. I knew she'd come up with a hustle that included us setting up shop somewhere to get me some money for school. I was still mad, but I had to give it to her. When Barbeque Bobbi set up shop, the neighborhood McDonalds and Popeyes felt the heat in lost sales. Besides, she had it all planned out, right down to being set up across the street right in front of the currency exchange on check day. She'd told the neighborhood guys, mostly my cousins, that for two weeks they had to buy food from us. Then she picked out a barely there Enyce shorts set and said, "Here, put this on. This will get the cars to stop." Well, some of them just blew their horns, but some of them stopped too, so I guess I was pre-internet click bait.

Nevertheless, we made enough money for my Mother to get my Aunt to drive me down to Dillard. I arrived on campus a few days later and made my way straight to the financial aid office to tell them to put me on the waiting list for housing or else I'd be sleeping in the library until we could figure out something. All I knew was that I couldn't go back home. Mama made that crystal clear right before we left to hit the road. She told me, "Go and do well 'cause if you don't, you don't have nowhere to come back to." My Aunt thought it was harsh, but it gave me the fuel to stay the course.

I didn't have time to be playing around and partying. College was serious for me and my future depended on my succeeding in school. By the second month, I had a job at the currency exchange down the street from campus and in the spirit of my Grandfather and Mama, I set up a late night snack bar called Munchies straight from my dorm room. My roommate Ena from Atlanta was cool as a fan. Her hustle was braiding hair. Our slogan was "Get your hair did and eat good too" because the cost of the hairstyle included a large nacho and cold drink (we call it pop in Chicago). This was my very first time branding a business and service and I didn't even realize it at first, but it made me consider Marketing as my major. New Orleans was like New York for me ... If I could make it there, the Chicago bravado in me would allow me to make it anywhere.

Now, I was very serious about school, but there was no way I couldn't have some fun in arguably the most fun city on the planet. The most musical memory of my college years wasn't the Bunny Hop or the NOLA Clap or even the Casper Cha Slide, although they did get a whole lot of play. I had come home to change clothes between school and work. We had left the TV on. Just as I was about to head out the door, I heard Common's voice say, "These are the stories told by Stony and Cottage Grove!" Wait a minute now! I ran to the TV and there it was, a video displaying some of the beauty that was Chicago from the El Train to familiar streets like 47th Street and he incorporated poetry too. I was in love—with the song, not Rasheed. He's attractive, but Tiffany Haddish is my homegirl (in my head 'cause she just ain't met me yet) and that's against the sister code. I got a noise violation that day from screaming Chi-town about 20 times, but it was so worth it.

Now that I had a job and a hustle, it was time for me to choose a major. Dillard didn't have a pre-law program so I wasn't sure what to choose at first. Urban Studies & Public Policy sounded fairly close to my interests so I enrolled in an introduction to Urban Studies course. We started studying communities like where I grew up and the history of housing projects and restrictive covenants. Yep, I was definitely in the right class and it was Urban Studies for me!

God sends you a source of inspiration in the depths of the valley. One day I was leaving my intro to Urban Studies class and took the long walk towards the pond to gather my thoughts. Just as I was leaving the trailers turned classrooms, I happened to glance at the resource board and noticed something new, an article with a familiar and striking image. The highlighted words jumped out at me, Ariel Mutual Funds Chicago, Appointed As President by John Rogers. I couldn't recall where I recognized the woman from, but I knew I had seen her a few times. I read the name aloud … Mellody Hobson and boom it hit me. She was a mentor during my grammar school years through the Big Shoulders Scholarship Fund that afforded me the chance to attend Holy Angels Catholic School! I remembered how eloquently she spoke and that she was a graduate of Princeton. Looking at the highlights of her recent accomplishments gave me the fuel to kick my determination into overdrive.

Just as I got done connecting the dots, one of my professors said, "See that Chicago inspiration for ya!" I proudly said, "Yep, and I know her too!" He gave me a "yeah right" look and jokingly said, "Andrea, you know all of Chicago and I guess you lived in Cabrini Green too." I quickly corrected him and said, "I ain't never lived nowhere near the westside and we only lived in the projects for two years before my Mama hustled her way out of there." I told him about the scholarship program and how Hobson became my mentor. He said, "Oh, you do know her! You think she'll remember you?" I said, "Maybe. I think I am memorable." He laughed and said, "Well, reach out to her then, Ms. Chicago." I walked off thinking, "Maybe I will." Now, that maybe is definitely! #AUDACITY

I had been doing my nails and feet all school year. After work I decided to treat myself to a pedicure at a nail shop across the street from the currency exchange. One of the gentlemen recognized me from his weekly trips to get money orders and send money to China. He greeted me with, "What's up wodie?!" It was a New Orleans friendly slang term, but he and I weren't that friendly and I found it to be offensive and unprofessional. I said, "My name is Andrea or Ms. Thompson. I'm no wodie." He seemed to take offense when I didn't accept his overtures, but it is what it is.

Shortly after sitting down, I started chatting with the sister in the next seat. The nail techs were speaking a different language, and I was pretty sure they were talking about Sis's feet. Then I noticed that the TV was on a station that wasn't in English. That's when I knew I had to say something (in my Adele Givens voice; shout out to *The Queens of Comedy*)! As politely as I could, I asked, "Can you turn to a station we all can understand since none of your clients can understand what's playing on TV?"

He looked even more offended than he was to my objection to being called wodie, but he grudgingly turned the channel.

As soon as he turned the station, I heard "E2 night club tragedy in Chicago." Tears came to my eyes as I saw graphic images of people trapped in the doorway—the same doorway I stood at and got access denied just a week before while home on break. I had tried to use my cousin's ID and couldn't remember all of her info. All I could do then was pray and call home to check on my people. This time my family was okay, but 21 people didn't make it back home to their families. The youngest was 19 years old and the oldest was 43. According to ABC 7 Chicago, the tragedy started "when security guards used pepper spray to break up a fight at the nightclub. People who tried to escape down a staircase got trampled and crushed to death." This unfortunately would not be the first or last time that tragedy was interwoven into the stories of residents of Chicago, but there is a resiliency about us that gives us the ability to keep on pushing when we really feel like giving up the fight.

I could probably write a book about my time at Dillard, and who knows I may, but somehow, almost as quickly as it started, it was over. My Aunt wanted me to leave my "lil' raggedy" car there and ride back with them. Well, I didn't know a whole lot but I knew two things for certain. One, I wasn't doing a road trip with them and, two, I wasn't leaving my lil' green Pontiac Sunfire that I paid for with my own hard-earned money. I got me some sleep and a tune-up and hit the road the next day. I drove all the way home on some Kanye, playing "Jesus Walks" while praying that Jesus would take the wheel. I had made it to graduation, but *The College Dropout* album on repeat got me up that road back to Chicago with a pit stop at Granny's house in Conway, Arkansas. Oh and not only did my lil' raggedy car get me to Chicago, it took me to Schaumburg where I got my first property management job.

My rent on a two-bedroom in Chicago was going to be about $300 more than the mortgage Granny paid on a three-bedroom house! I wish somebody had told me to buy that house from Granny. If I knew what I know now ... but I was young and city life was calling me so I doubt I would have seen the vision of exchanging big city excitement for forest in the country life.

## Connection Clue

What things did you believe about yourself that you had to dispel and think about differently in order to create different outcomes?

Are there some people in your close circle who could possibly pose major liabilities (thwarting your path to success) if they don't change, or you don't eliminate them from your inner circle?

What subpar treatment are you tolerating? What relationships are you maintaining where your presence is being tolerated and not necessarily appreciated?

Is there a terrorist alert that you need to address in order to operate with keen discernment and peace? This could be a toxic relationship, an unhealthy addiction, or a self-limiting thought that you affirm by giving it credence.

What attributes does your circle need to reflect to support where you are going in your higher destiny and goals? Assess your current circle in comparison to what you need to give and receive from your closest connections. Some relationships may have to change. Others may become non-existent. That's okay, and it may not be either person's fault. It's just a new step towards your destiny.

**"I wanted to surround myself with the kind of people who could help me turn my life around; people whom I could rub up against like iron and be sharpened."—Eric "ET" Thomas**

| Attributes of your current circle | Attributes of your desired circle |
| --- | --- |
| | |
| | |

| Attributes of your current circle | Attributes of your desired circle |
|---|---|
| | |
| | |
| | |
| | |
| | |
| | |
| | |
| | |
| | |

**Audacity Affirmation**

I am connected to amazing people who genuinely want to see me win. I am attracting mutually beneficial relationships. I am realigning or removing connections that are self-serving, toxic or counterproductive. My crew is growing with me, and we are dynamic, loyal and full of promise.

# Chapter 2

# The Gift in the Gab

A man's gift maketh room for him,
and bringeth him before great men.
Proverbs 18:16

From a very early age, I knew I could talk or rather that I had the "gift of the gab." Of course, "just talking" and actually saying something significant are two different things. A colleague once angrily said to me: "You don't take pictures or video; all you got is the gift of the gab." I am in media, so I can definitely appreciate the skillset of photographers and videographers. Nevertheless, what I discovered in working with some of them is that they are often only equipped to operate in their specific zone of genius.

It was a benefit and enhancement to their operations to have a point of contact for initial inquiries who also facilitated pre-shoot directions and post-shoot delivery of content in a seamless way that provided optimum customer service. Then the photographer only needed to receive an email with pertinent details about time, project type, location and point of contact. I automatically changed so many of the emails and inbox language to a more professional tone. I literally took it from, "Yeah, what day you trying to book for?" to "Thank you so much for considering us to capture your special event. Let's start with the date and time and we'll confirm our availability before sending a form to give us more information to serve you best." Of course the second response spoke to a different clientele and justified a price increase.

After I processed and showed the value I brought to the business process, I started to really think about the true gift the "gift of the gab" is. Communication is a major gift. It is the foundation and conclusion of every business deal. Without communication, how can any work be properly executed? What you say is important, and even more important is how you say it, and WHO you say it to. I heard a Southern belle say: "You can't share everything with everybody because they may not be equipped to carry the weight." Indeed, you can be saying all the right things, but the words will render themselves useless and die at the ear of the wrong person. Don't bring a live message to a dead place and wonder if your words were wrong. No, your choice of audience was wrong. By the same token, the right person will take your words and be impacted, inspired or called to action.

What are you saying and who are you saying it to? This is one of the key things I've taught in many marketing sessions. It's also very applicable in life overall. If you share international, big vision dreams with someone who is afraid to travel by air, they will only be able to relate based on their experience with ground transportation. The traveling experience by bus is so different from the luxury of first-class air travel. That is not to look down or frown upon ground travel, but there are some places that are only accessible by air!

Being in the air gives you an overview to overstand how interconnected things truly are. I've had some of my best thoughts studying for school, writing exams, or working on business plans while 30,000 miles in the sky, ascending at a rapid rate to reach a destination for a greater purpose. The airport experience was even a part of my writing process for this book. Portions of this book were written midflight and in airports between connecting flights.

I first discovered that I had a real gift for public speaking when I spoke at the funeral of the neighborhood big mama who was like my grandmother. Her daughters were like my aunties and one of them was my godmother. Without a pen and paper, and not even much forethought as to what I would say, I stepped to the podium and started speaking straight from my heart, recollecting the advice she'd given me and the love she'd shown me. Somehow, I was only nervous for the first few words and then they just started flowing smoothly as if I had prepared and practiced a speech. After the service, a couple people—distant family members I had never met—asked what I did. I said, "Oh, I'm just a manager at a car rental company trying to afford law school." Some of the Southern ladies said, "Well, gon' baby, you'd be good at that. You gon' make it." I smiled and said, "Thank you," but not really believing, while my side-eye, shade-throwing cousin gave me a cynical, envious grin.

You know it ain't cool to shine among darkness; the glare from your shine provokes their snare. I'd learned early on and mostly during college that when I came around certain people and environments, I had to dim my light or dumb myself down. (I no longer do that, but the pressure to dim your shine is a book in itself!)

Anyway, in that moment of speaking passionately through pain, with my voice shaking slightly and tears running down my cheeks, I felt like God was crafting my story, a living testimony, and He was strengthening my voice to speak on it once I got to the other side of the pain. Speaking and sharing your story in a real and authentic way is having the resolve to say: "This happened to me and there was a lesson and a blessing." Sharing the story and the painful parts of the path can be a blueprint for someone else's healing and more importantly, it can let them know that healing is in fact possible.

**"We all go through pain; get a reward for it."**

**—Eric "ET" Thomas**

It took writing this book to remind me of the first time my block brothers nicknamed me Oprah. I didn't like it at first and wanted them to just call me by my family nickname, Nikki. Later though, I was curious and asked them why they called me that.

They said it was because I was "preaching to the people and I needed my own talk show." I had been called lil' Angela Davis at summer camp, but Oprah seemed to stick until the Michael Jackson documentary. Out of disappointment with Lady O, my cousin, (who I affectionately call "Cuzzy Wuzzy"), renamed me ... drum roll ... Michelle Obama! That's three great women who unknowingly gave me permission to step into my own unique greatness with even more audacity!

Chicago festivals and community events are some of the best memories I have of growing up on the south side. The KOCO Fest was like a smaller version of the Bud Billiken Parade, but it packed a wow of its own. Once a year, I'd wait to hear the sirens from an old station wagon going down Drexel Boulevard screaming over a bullhorn, "It's KOCO Fest Day!" There was one year my cousins talked about for years. I was about seven, and although I wasn't vocally talented enough to sing, I wanted to go on stage so I stood in line with the other performers. When the talent show host gave me the mic, I didn't know what to say so I said, "My name is Nikki. I'm trying to find my Mama and Daddy." Almost in concert, several people started laughing like I'd told a joke. The host thought they didn't hear me and said, "Alright now, y'all, we have a lost and found baby up here." One of the aunties spit out her beer laughing before belting out, "That's Bobbi and dem baby. She ain't lost. She lives in that building right there across the street." Then she turned her smirk into a stern, "Nikki get yo' lil' ass off that stage."

I gave the mic back, but I stayed on the side of the stage watching the production from the sidelines. I didn't know what a run of show was but I was paying attention to who was running the show. I also didn't know yet that I wanted to do anything in film, media or marketing. I only knew that I liked writing and wanted to be a lawyer.

Years later when I was in law school and did my first live on Facebook, my cousin who had taught me the perils of shining too hard called me and said, "Damn, first you was Oprah. Now you Barbara Walters!" Well, I'll take that too—the Black Barbara Walters. Andrea Monique Thompson is fine too!

## The Early Seeds of Entrepreneurship: Five Swirls

I window-shopped houses in Hyde Park, but when it came to window-shopping clothes, downtown State Street and Michigan Avenue were my go-to spots. I'd go on to work at FAO Schwarz, a luxury version of Toys 'R' Us. I really just wanted the discount to shop for my little sisters for Christmas, but even with a discount those toys were high. On my lunch break I'd window shop at the Escada store, the Water Tower and sometimes St. John's. I was so happy to learn that there was a black woman designer, Mai Rai, nearby. She made everybody's prom dresses and when my time came, I wanted her to make mine too. My last stop on the window shopper's route was always Roberto's where I would learn about fine leathers, including Davocci coats that later became referred to as "drug dealer" coats. It's funny because these jackets inspired me to get my first job, but when I got my check and saw how many checks I'd need to buy one, I kinda lost interest!

After I got tired of looking at stuff I couldn't buy, I'd end my downtown adventure at the Sports McDonalds where I'd get my regular: a chicken nugget happy meal with an apple pie and an ice-cream cone if I had enough money. I had been there plenty of times doing my homework on the second floor at the same table by the window. That day, I got the bright idea that I needed to see about getting a job there. I figured out who the manager was and when I saw him passing by I said, "Yo tengo necessita trabajar. Yo es muy bien estudiente. Ayudar?" He looked at me surprised. I figured speaking in his native language would make me stand out among other applicants. It worked because he gave me an application and told me to bring it back the next week for an interview. I dressed in my Sunday best, topped off with my best set of pearls. I had even researched some of the history of McDonalds. I was ready and within the first 15 minutes of the interview, I had my first job offer as a part-time front line cashier! My joy was almost short-lived when Hugo put my date of birth in the computer and the screen flashed red saying "underage." Apparently I was nearly two years short of the age requirement! Hugo turned to me and said,

"You're 16 if anyone asks, ¿¡Sí!?"—to which I quickly responded, "Sí Sí, yo comprehende."

I got an early education in production costs and customer service when one day, the owner, Mr. Cirelo McSween happened to stop by to check in and noticed I was doing five swirls on the soft-serve ice-cream cones instead of three. He instructed me to count one, two, three and then stop. I eyed him as I thought giving people a big, fat ice-cream cone the way I'd want my own cone was the best customer service. Later that day, 60644's own, Da Brat, walked up to my register. She ordered a Sprite and an ice-cream cone. I caught Mr. McSween eyeing me as I was thinking, "Come on now! She's Da Brat." But that didn't seem to faze him from his 3-swirl limit.

A few weeks later, I was in trouble again. Mr. McSween caught me giving away food to homeless people at the end of my shift. I just knew it was the end of the road for me and Mickey D's when he said, "Why would you give away my food?" I replied, "People are hungry and we would have just thrown it away anyway." He paused, seeming to consider what I'd said. Then he finally responded, "Okay, but only once a week!" I was surprised and grateful that he didn't fire me and I'm sure the people that I fed were pleased with his decision too.

Not too long after though, I decided I couldn't take the heat in the kitchen after nearly a week without A/C. I called before I came in to work to see if the air was back on. It wasn't so I quit and went right across the street to the DePaul University bookstore and got another job before you could finish saying ice-cream cone. I went and ate lunch at my old job and told a couple of my former co-workers that I'd traded in burgers for books. One of them came over and got a job at the bookstore too!

Unfortunately, years later I heard that Hugo was killed by a drug cartel in Mexico! I also learned more about Cirilo McSween and his humble beginnings as well as his influence on the Black McDonalds Association. McSween's Foundation continues to pour into the African-American community, and that is definitely something I feel passionate about. His story is one that is more than audacious!

## Grooming & Brooming

It's interesting how experiences make you reflect on your own responses in certain situations. I had reached out to a young lady who had recently completed school to ask if she was interested in a paid opportunity to assist me with my brand. Without hesitation she said that she really didn't have much time because she was building her own brand. I thought it would be advantageous to work on the client accounts I had that were associated with 20-year-veteran business owners, giving her access and exposure with pay. And I thought to myself, "What happened to paying your dues?" Well maybe the young people were on to something ... to bet it on all on themselves from the get-go.

This led me to reflect on my own misperceptions or misgivings about business in my 20s. Case in point, my first transportation position was in a management trainee role at a neighborhood branch in Hyde Park before I graduated to the airport. The best part for me was that I got to pick up scheduled car rentals from some of the city's business leaders from marketing execs, publicity managers and financial consultants to CEOs and singers. During one of my rides, I sparked up a conversation with an amazing woman who happened to be the owner of a lucrative liquor store that was her family business. The next time I picked her up, she gifted me with tickets to the Mary J. Blige and Jay-Z concert and gave me the connect for an interview when I told her I needed a second job as I was eventually planning to leave my car rental role.

A couple months later, I was working at the liquor store and although I was grateful for my second opportunity to learn from a black business owner, I felt like the position was a major fall from the privileges they told me earning a degree would bestow upon me. I had let the shady words of my older cousin who said, "All that college don't mean nothing if you end up working any kind of job" make me feel out of alignment in my position. Truth be told, I wanted a glamorous downtown office, but I ended up processing rental contracts and working at a liquor store. One night I was asked to sweep the floor and with foolish audacity I said, "That's not in my job description." In hindsight, now that I'm a business owner, if I need to sweep the floor, I'll be the best lil' sweeper you've ever seen. I thought after Sallie Mae my dues were paid, but I found out I'm still paying them (Word to Jadakiss)! I didn't yet realize the practical skills that I needed to learn nor the fundamentals and building blocks of creating a success story, but I've learned to use every opportunity as a brick in the foundation of what I'm building with God's grace.

## The Help and the Helpless

I had taken a temporary job at a private membership club downtown right off of Lake Shore Drive. I enrolled in a fine dining and alcohol serving training course after I mispronounced crème brûlée at a business event. I also knew knowledge of wines and traditional top-shelf drinks was another important basic. I thought this would be a good way to put that to use while I looked for another job in the transportation industry. Just like when I went to the private plane's smaller airport when working at Midway, the only black and brown faces were people who worked there. I made it my business to ask the woman who had been working there the longest, Ms. Lucille, if there were any black members at the Knightly Estate. She said there was only one, a black woman who lives in Africa. She told me she is said to be as rich as Oprah, but she only came in about once a year.

Ms. Lucille was from Jamaica and we grew fond of each other. We'd talk over our lunch break, mostly about our families and being a mother. When she found out I wanted to go to law school, she seemed interested in talking about that and my time in New Orleans for undergrad. I soon noticed how she spoke when Jill, the house property manager came around. She and the other employees always had a joke for her or a compliment on her outfit or accessories. I didn't do the most with Jill. I simply said hello and you could tell she didn't like my neutral engagement. She clearly wanted me to express more excitement when she came into the room, but I didn't see the need. I was there to do a job not kiss up to people. I was a couple years younger than her, had just as much education and like her I'd worked in property management for years. That job was temporary and I wasn't about to start talking like I was in the 1850s to stroke her ego.

Aside from Ms. Lucille, I started to make an unlikely connection with a white colleague named Jane. She was an undergraduate student around 21 or 22. We started talking about her application to grad school. When I mentioned my Notre Dame acceptance, she seemed both shocked and impressed. When we got around to the topic of her getting her first job, just as I suspected, her Dad knew some of the members and got her a job with one phone call. My journey was different. I had to go through two in-person interviews and a phone interview.

One day Jane came to work more joyful than usual. She said, "Andrea, I found my ring!" I said, "Girl, I didn't even know you'd gotten engaged.

Congratulations!" She said, "No, I'm not ... not yet." I said, "You think your boyfriend might ask?" She said, "I'm not serious with anyone right now, but my Daddy said it was time for me to get a job and a husband to take care of me. He got me the job. Now it's time to find my man."

She whipped out her phone and proudly showed me a huge rock before saying, "Talk about bling-bling." I gave her a look like, "Don't go too far homegirl." I looked closely and said, "The clarity and quality is nice. How many carats is it?" I wanted her to know I knew the language of diamonds beyond "bling-bling" (Pass the Grey Poupon). She said, "Almost 20k worth." With controlled facial expressions, I asked, "What if the man that finds you can't afford it?" Without hesitation, she replied, "Oh if he can't, then he is not the one! Daddy told me to get a man who can take care of me on the level he does or better and I won't settle for anything less."

Hmmm, I quickly got tired of talking to Jane and went back to folding napkins with Ms. Lucille, but later that evening when I got home to my man and his roommate, Lil' Man, I had to give Jane's comments further consideration. Was Jane considered to be a gold digger or did she just have high standards? It's interesting that some women are going half on light bills and doing everything they can to keep a man happy who can barely take care of himself let alone her and the family. Looking for cheese/cheddar doesn't make a woman a hood rat ... word to Common.

Let's normalize black women living luxuriously, and, yes, let's normalize having standards that include financial stability. Let me be clear, money isn't everything, but it answers all things. That's Biblical. The richness of my legacy and what my children inherit is directly impacted by the man I will marry and the last name I take so no I will not be your ride and die when I was created to fly and flourish. I deserve the best and you do too, Sis. That's on baby, Mary and the lil' lamb too.

While we are talking about standards, let's talk about the rather alarming trend of rating and berating black women who have standards. During the creation of this book, I discovered there is a huge gulf in the percentages of white women who marry versus black women—it's about a 50% difference. The reasons cited for that are generally underemployment and incarceration of black men. What happens though as a result of this "shortage" is the idea that you should just take what you can get. There's also a feeling that women who want financial stability as well as love and loyalty are asking for too much. I just hit the over 35 mark and have one son, but it is still my feeling and my hope that beautiful, bountiful Black love is still possible for both men and women.

Back to my "Help" experience though, my most memorable travel back in time moment was when we were preparing the space for the wedding of one of the member's daughters. There was no one in the house, apart from staff. I went to the restroom on the first floor because it was closest to the presidential room where I was setting the table. One of the other servers walked past and saw me at the sink washing my hands. You would have thought she'd seen a ghost. As she gasped and clutched her imaginary pearls, she said, "Get out of there Andrea! We're only allowed to use the basement bathroom." Startled by how overly offended she seemed to be, "I said there are no guests in the house." She said, "It doesn't matter. Just come out and wash your hands before James comes and sees you in there." They really called him the overseer, in a joking way, but I didn't find it to be funny, especially since they were doing their best to look like they were being casted for the Chicago version of *The Help*. I was really trying to make the best of it and not rock the boat, but I was never really good at going along with anything just to get along and my speaking out often not only rocked the boat but often led to a *Titanic* experience.

The wedding came and I was assigned to a table of 10 to serve. One of the gentlemen at the table was having a conversation about law school and his undergraduate school, Notre Dame. We had a Notre Dame room upstairs so I said, "Did you know there is a room on the house's third level named after the university?" That led to me talking about law school and within two or three minutes he introduced me to his wife, who was as an alum as well and he gave me her card. He genuinely seemed interested in offering advice. Well, one of my colleagues told the lady house manager that I was "fratinizing" with a guest and got his number, implying that I was being inappropriate somehow.

Ms. Lucille seemed to always know what was going on at the house. In fact, she knew I was fired before I knew. She said, "I knew you weren't going to last long here." I said, "That's what my Mama said too. Why you say that Ms. Lucille?" She replied, "You too strong, and they don't like that, but I admire that about you. You'd make a good lawyer. Take my number honey and you keep in touch."

Sure enough, the next thing I knew, James started acting really nervous when I asked him about the next week's schedule. Jill wanted to schedule a meeting with me, and I'd already made up my mind that I wasn't about to bow down and kiss the ring. I opted to email because sometimes I speak too sharply. Therefore, a professionally polished email is often a better option. Needless to say, I was fired and they told me to keep the uniforms and they'd mail my last check. That was cool with me, as I had an interview coming up anyway. A few years later when I started my business, I had the audacity to put my own brand on those same uniforms. There was no need for them to go to waste so I made them my own. Yep, my first initial is A. For audacity!

Cadillac made its own audacious statement with its "Audacity of Blackness" campaign. My marketing mind and my experience in the transportation industry led me to study the advertising and longevity of one of the longest surviving automotive brands, Cadillac. Although I grew to like the Infiniti, having worked at one of their dealerships, the Cadillac brand speaks to a luxury lifestyle that appeals to a particular audience they have cultivated by knowing how to pivot powerfully leading with a custom touch powered by innovation. Indeed marketing is like a car. Where are you going? What's driving you? What message are you sending?

## First Class

When I hosted my first business conference in downtown Chicago on the Mag Mile, I was still attending law school on the West Coast, but I knew that if I couldn't yet afford tickets to get into the rooms I wanted to enter, I needed to use my resources to create rooms so that I could get exposure, knowledge and connections. The first year POWBIZ Conference was a woman's business event. I had eight speakers including "Sinclair" from the hit sitcom, *Living Single*! Luckily, she was coming in from nearby Ohio. I had other speakers coming from as far as Florida and Cali.

My most challenging encounter came from the headliner. Her first concern was that her picture was not as big as the celebrity guest's picture. Then she demanded that we fly her first class. I mean it wasn't like we were flying her on spiritless; she was flying the friendly skies with my favorite premium airline. But she didn't want that. She insisted that we fly her first class on one of two carriers that she preferred.

At that stage, I didn't know enough to incorporate a non-compete exclusivity clause in the performance contract, so she ended up having her own separate event in the same hotel I was staying in for the event at $200 per ticket. This obviously adversely impacted my ticket sales, and I basically flew her there for her event. To her, my event was "get something on the side." Well Played by her and Lesson Learned by me.

Although I'd taken a course in contracts, it took this situation to force me to learn about restrictive clauses to prevent things like that from leaving you with talent that oversaturates the market. Business can be brutal and I quickly realized that the hustle and always seeing the grind gave me transferable skills, especially in sales and marketing. However, as I grew I realized that the hustle will leave you exhausted. At some point, multiple streams of passive income and products versus services have to come into play. After all, there are only 24 hours in the day and if you're spending most of them working, all you're doing is trading in your 9 to 5 for a 9 to 9.

For the second year of the conference, I decided that it was important to include men in the discussions. It wasn't so much that organizing the women got on my nerves as it was that far too often men were sorely outnumbered at professional events when their presence and perspective was too needed and valued to not be included. This is also why I made a conscious decision to include men in the audacious discussions on relationships in my

Clubhouse room. We can learn a lot from each other, if we only take the time to *really* listen.

## Connection Clue

What is something that you have been struggling with, something that is painful and perhaps hindering you from accomplishing your goals and having a better quality of life? What teachable moments have you had during your valley moments?

Reflect on what measures you took to push through, and what skills you used to navigate the difficulty of that situation. Maybe you developed a new skill or learned more about yourself.

Your first concern might not be writing to document a challenge while you're working to overcome it, but I can tell you this for sure, if you write even when it hurts the most, you not only put the pain on the paper but you leave a "gladiator's guide" that helps others know that they can GITUP too. Turn the inspiration to energy!

**I had few to no role models for what I came to do professionally as a leadership consultant and business owner, but I had faith and the audacity to walk through every door God opened for me. And God has opened many doors and brought me into relationships with people who have allowed me to teach, train and speak across the U.S. and at least sixteen other countries.**

**The journey has not been without its challenges but one thing I'm clear on is this: the Lord is the Ultimate Plug for me and keeps me connected to my purpose of serving others.—Dr. Jeanne Porter King**

## Connecting the dots

What would the breakthrough story of your life look like? Go further: what would it FEEL like? Sketch it out. Write the story. Record yourself speaking it. You often have to envision it before you can achieve it. Write it and make it plain.

**Audacity Affirmation**

I will use my voice powerfully, declaring that I am going to use all of my gifts, treasures and talents boldly and impactfully. I won't be silenced, if I choose to speak. But even when silent, my silence can make a statement.

# Chapter 3

## At Gunpoint: Uncovered Yet Kept

The LORD is nigh unto them that are of a broken heart; and saveth such as be of a contrite spirit.
Psalm 34:18

Wanting to get out became NEEDING to get out, but I felt stuck—stuck with a mean man who didn't love himself enough to love me or maybe he only loved himself. I had moved into the home afforded to him by his sugar mama who had been recently incarcerated for Federal fraud charges. To make matters worse, his roommate "Little Man" was staying there too and started telling me the "rules of the house" like it was his to be the boss of. I felt so low, so unprotected and I was for sure sleeping with the enemy. His friend didn't have respect for me because he witnessed him disrespecting me.

It wasn't always bad. We grew up together, and I even used to run away to his Mom's house. We had known each other since basketball on crates and double dutch days. He had always been my *Love & Basketball* and I was his "SpottieOttieDopaliscious" like the OutKast song. He reminded me of a cross between Jadakiss and Twista. I was diggin' it. He was smooth with his words and that was what made me weak. I didn't know that eventually his words would literally make me weak, not from being so romantic that they swept me off my feet, but that he'd use his words to belittle and break me in such major ways.

While I was pregnant, I had noticed how eyes would go from my growing belly to my left hand, especially at church, so I felt honored when my childhood sweetheart presented me with a diamond ring. He didn't ask for my hand in marriage or anything really. He simply said, "I love you and always have" and then he presented me with a little red box. He'd given me his Grandmother's ring when we were kids and asked me to marry him then, but we were only teenagers. The ring symbolized hope … until we had an argument and he blurted out that the sugar mama had bought that too! You could have sold me for a penny and got change. Somehow I ended up in a soap opera with no idea of what I had signed up for, and I for darn sure did not know my lines. I was speechless.

I have to take responsibility for my part in staying in a toxic relationship. Our strongest bond was a trauma bond. Those are often the hardest to break, but they are the ones we must break if we are to ever heal or move forward. I knew without a doubt he was a master of manipulation when he blamed me when he got caught cheating. Devasted I said, "I don't know how I can forgive you." Without hesitation, he said, "The same way you forgave your father."

This particular morning we got into an argument as we often did. He grabbed his keys and stormed out. I foolishly ran after him. He pulled off and left me standing there in the middle of the street at 3 am. I couldn't stop crying. I wished my life was different. I truly loved that man who said the most hurtful things and was almost as mean as my Dad. In fact, he was strangely similar to him. I felt stupid for choosing him when I knew the complete opposite of my Dad would have put me in a better position than the struggle love I'd become accustomed to. I knew if I went home I would only cry and sleep. My son was with my Grandma so I decided I would go to sunrise service. I needed something to affirm me as everything around me was rooted in rejection that denied me joy and robbed me of peace. I was coming out of post-partum depression, and I also wanted to let go of toxic relationships: friendship, family and this man included. I had to re-evaluate everyone because withdrawals without deposits will leave you bankrupt and overdrawn.

Normally very watchful of my surroundings, I was thrown off. I was literally walking down the street with tears streaming down my face. To be honest, I wasn't even really concerned about my safety. I felt barely alive. I walked to the gas station and saw a man turn the corner ahead of me. As I walked behind him, I saw two young boys on bicycles. In what seemed like a matter of a couple a seconds, one of the boys got in front of the man who was ahead of me and pulled out a gun, telling him to empty his pockets. I stopped in my tracks and quickly realized I couldn't run. The other boy had dropped his bike and said, "You too Bitch." I dropped the glass juice bottle I was holding and put my hands up. He put the gun to my head. I had been scared of guns since seeing my high school friend dead at the county hospital, but for some reason unbeknownst to me a sense of slight calm came over me. I still can't explain why, but I waved my hand across my face in such a way that the gun was then at my shoulder. The gun could have went off, but I reasoned I would rather it be in the shoulder.

As I motioned, I pleaded with him. I said, "Naw come on, it can't go like this. I have a son. My son will be one next week. Please." He pushed me up against the black iron fence, grabbed my breast and then my vagina. I told myself, "Just breathe. This has happened before, but you've never been shot before. You can survive that kind of taking." He stopped when he heard his buddy tell the guy that was being robbed to get out of there. The man looked back at me as he ran off, like he almost felt sorry for me, but knew there was nothing he could do.

The boy stepped back and pointed the gun at my chest again. All I could say was one word, "God." He said, "Open that bag. What you got for me?" I reached inside my big tote bag without looking and the first thing I grabbed was the custom invites to my son's first birthday party. I held his picture up to the boy and said, "Look at my baby. My son needs me. Please don't take me away from him." He looked me right in the eye and said, "A'ight, just empty out the bag and we gonna let you go lil' mama." I thought, "I wasn't a lil' mama; I was somebody's mama." I emptied out the whole bag on the ground. He took my phone and the $20 in cash and hopped back on his bike like nothing had happened.

I walked to the gas station on the corner in a trance. It seemed like I was floating. When I got there, I asked to use the phone and they could tell without me explaining that something bad had happened to me. Before I even called the police, I called my so-called man. I just wanted him to know that his carelessness for me had left me hurt and unprotected yet again. He said, "I'm on my way" and hung up. I called the police next. By the time I got done with the report, my man's friend was walking up asking if I was okay. Shortly after that, my boyfriend pulled up and told me to get in.

As soon as I got in the car, I called my Mom from his phone and through sniffles and tears, I recounted the occurrence to her. The first words she said stuck with me, "Calm down Nikki. At least he didn't rape you." I replied, "It felt almost as bad." I felt terrible that it took such an extreme for even an expression of empathy as if what was done didn't rise to a standard that warranted my tears. Her responses were almost condescending, like: "That's all and you crying about that?"

As we went back "home," I knew I wanted out … out of situations with mean men who hurt me and didn't protect me, out of connections to toxic family members and out of this violent city. I wanted to move away from it all. I started making plans little by little to detach from what I finally knew and felt without a doubt just wasn't right. I deserved so much more. Even if I didn't see it in any form around me, I was set on believing that better existed somewhere and somehow. And I wanted to feel it.

My empathy and compassion for my son's father as an unfathered father could not come at the expense of my peace. His healing could absolutely not come to fruition as a result of my being broken. I deserved peace and would not be made to live in pieces—fragmented versions of my greatest potential left unmanifested, burdened by betrayal, crippled by fear. I knew that I couldn't become under his hand so I put myself in God's hands.

I wanted to be angry at him forever, but I knew I had to forgive him someday. I was sick and tired of mean men! I'd known them my whole life. They'd say things to break me, put me down, demean, and handle or rather mishandle me. I hadn't really known love and hadn't really seen it, not the kind of love that was devoid of hurt. I had only seen love that would make one not even want to choose it. I used to think that hitting me was the worst because of the old lie, "Sticks and stones may break my bones, but words will never hurt me." As a wordsmith, I know words can build you up, but they can also tear you down, leaving you with wounds that take years to heal.

And just in case anyone is wondering, I knew he wasn't my husband, but I thought I should make a child with him. Uh oh, the praise dancers have halted and the organ has paused! Wait a minute, let me explain. I had always wanted to be a Mom. I just wasn't sure about being a wife. I know that most women dream of the fairytale wedding. I didn't because I saw what it looked like after the wedding. I loved weddings ... and I mean everything about them from the cake to the throwing of the bouquet that I've never seen a woman even let touch the floor. However, I also noticed how reluctant the men were when the groom throws the garter belt. They'd part like the Red Sea and leave that thing on the floor like it was a deadly predator. At my cousin's beachside wedding, I was around 12 or 13. They had to practically drag that man down the aisle. It took them two hours of going in the room talking to him just to get him to come out over an hour late! The truth is it seemed that men weren't excited about getting married and women weren't doing any better being married from what I was seeing so I figured,

"I can do bad by myself" like I'd heard some of my "ol' lady gang" say.

I was most definitely going through a strong battle with postpartum depression, working 60 hours a week, and trying to figure out how to make my next move. I remembered when he told me that he wouldn't stray if I was taking care of home. Hell, we didn't even have a home! I had a place and he had a sugar mama. I stayed, tried and cried, mainly because I didn't feel like anyone else would want me. I was broken and I doubted every part of me. I wasn't my best self with him, but I was afraid to leave because I wasn't sure who I was without him.

As time wore on though, for the first time I realized that mental and emotional abuse could be far more damaging than physical abuse. His words and how low they made me feel often came to revisit me even during my temporary moments of escape. I made a small move at first to a suburb two hours away. There wasn't a law school there, but I'd gotten a job at the biggest employer in town, a top insurance company. My aunt was a senior level executive there, but I had the same attitude I did in high school, "I can get my own job. I don't need nobody to put me on." It was half pride and half knowing that if I had to walk off the job I didn't want it to reflect poorly on her. I was a hard worker and a smart one, which made me a problem for HR because apparently knowing the policies and applying them made you a less malleable employee. I had no problem speaking out when I saw bias and would quit in a New York minute and storm out of the office in a Chicago winter. On the love ledger though, all I knew was that the boy I used to run to that made me feel safe was now the cause of my agony.

Love alone is not enough but without love nothing else is enough. People tap out at the bar when they've reached their limit. Many men seek to make you tap out in one way or another. But how many men can make a woman tap IN? Tap in to who she really is meant to be without feeling as if her being more somehow reduces their manhood.

## Connection Clue

Have you been through a lifesaving moment, or something life-altering that showed you the reality you were living was not the reality you envisioned? Maybe you're living it now.

What do you need to change? What steps do you need to take?

Ironically, it took a near-death experience to realize staying in a toxic relationship was actually already killing me, word by word, and day by day. It was killing my self-esteem, my energy and my dreams. I'm so thankful I made it out alive with the seeds to thrive by the grace of God.

**Audacity Affirmation**

I will love like I've never been hurt. I will have the courage to trust again and let down my guard in God's perfect timing. God does all things well and He loves best. I am love and I am loved.

# Chapter 4

## The Longest Flight Home

**"I have walked that long road to freedom. I have tried not to falter; I have made missteps along the way. But I have discovered the secret that after climbing a great hill, one only finds that there are many more hills to climb. I have taken a moment here to rest, to steal a view of the glorious vista that surrounds me, to look back on the distance I have come. But I can only rest for a minute, for with freedom come responsibilities, and I dare not linger, for my long walk is not ended."**

**—Nelson Mandela**

So, I'd never really been able to beat a boy up, but Lord knows I tried. I mean, I wasn't bullying boys, but I did not back down when provoked. I played almost all the sports the boys played, although football was out of my tomboy range. My cousin Lendy was the only female I knew that could straight handle men like she was a professional boxer. Her brother is 6'4" and muscular and they had a fight at a family outing one time and Cuz couldn't do nothing with Lendy. She was like Laila Ali to me. I wanted to learn how to fight like that so if a man, any man, ever beat me I'd be ready to take him down like the coward he was. My little cousin used to call me Catwoman because he said my eyes were slanted like a cat, but I wanted to be Catwoman because she was fine and she wasn't taking no butt whoopings. My Dad had told me that my mouth would get me knocked upside the head when I did get a boyfriend. Well, that didn't add up because I saw women who didn't always speak up for themselves still getting beat.

I knew I wanted a boyfriend at some point, but if he went upside my head, I didn't want to be one of those women who didn't fight back. How do you fight back though, knowing the odds are against you? I learned after the first couple of lover spats that turned physical that the only way to fight back was to put something in your hand to get them off of you. I remember so many times examining my face to assess the damage. I wanted to fight back, but I felt defeated. Even when I tried to leave, he'd be waiting outside my school or job with "I'm sorry" gifts. (He was sorry.) I wondered, "Did love always have to hurt so much?" I remember wishing that I didn't want love so badly because even when I became numb, I still wanted it desperately even at the expense of my self-esteem.

Having seen my share of heartbreaks, one in particular shook me as he had been my knight in shining armor. He had literally fought for me. I'd done everything I could to keep the football star happy, but he wanted me to transfer to his school in down state Illinois and as much as I missed him I knew I had to do me. He was on a full scholarship, got three meals a day and plenty of snacks. I was working at a currency exchange down the street from school, had a partial scholarship and sometimes my people slid their card to me so I could eat dinner on campus. I appreciated the money he sent and he constantly reminded me that he was gonna go pro one day, but I wasn't banking on that. I was no athlete but I thought, "Hell, imma go pro too!"

College definitely changed how he acted towards me. He went from being the top NFL prospect in the state and #1 at his high school to being "redshirted" his freshman year. For some reason he saw this as a bad thing because he rode the bench, but when I researched it I was like, "Uhm, this is a pretty good deal 'cause they'll pay for your first year of graduate school." He didn't see it that way.

Over the school year, he started drinking and hanging out with the really wild, blackout frat boys. He would drunk call me and ask if I was his "down ass bitch" when he had never called me that. I went to go see him after he complained that men have "needs." I hated hearing that and used to think, "What about what women need?" Folks seldom talk about that part.

When I went there, he wanted to do things in ways that we had never done. I told him I didn't want to. He was so drunk that he told on himself. He said, "It's a damn shame that I'm gonna go pro and you can't let me have you completely and how I want to when it's a couple white chicks I can call that'll let me do whatever I like." I just let him talk. I couldn't muster the strength to even give any backtalk. I didn't know about "Becky with the good hair" back then, but I let his words make me feel like I was inferior, when the real deal was that I was a Queen unseen. Even with my silence, he got madder saying, "Black bitches like you from the hood got a lot of mouth but need to know their place." He eventually got tired of ranting and ultimately said, "Do it or get out." Initially I refused to go until he got physical and then I didn't have a choice. I got out.

I called my grammar school friends that went to school there, but I was ashamed to tell them what had happened. I hung out with friends like I hadn't just gotten hit a few hours before. I managed to contain my feelings until the bus back to Chicago came. I took the back seat in the corner and I finally let out all the tears. It seemed like I'd cry all the way to Union Station, but 20 minutes in I had to tell myself the opposite of everything he had said to break me. I refused to go back to school in New Orleans broken and weeping so I had to spend the rest of the road trip building myself back up.

What's extra sad is that I didn't recognize verbal abuse as "real abuse" and the physical abuse was so isolated mainly because I was away most of the time. I had been beaten worse and I was used to mean words so none of it really seemed too far out of the norm. The devastating part is it had happened often enough that it almost felt normal.

Like so many women though, I still felt I could make him happy, not really thinking about whether making me happy even entered his mind. Even through the tears on the way back to school, I knew I would forgive him. But I wanted to make sure that I didn't feel inferior because of his words. I believed the mental anguish of that would be far more lasting than the chance of him hitting me. When we came home from school the next summer, I got a studio in Hyde Park so that we'd have a space of our own. Besides, my big brother had come home from jail and he and my nephew's Mom had taken my room.

I got my scholarship approved to study abroad. That was confirmation that the end of me and N'eres was near. My boss at the currency exchange in New Orleans had referred me for a job at a currency exchange in Chicago. It was right across the street from a liquor store and when N'eres picked me up with that brown paper bag I knew I'd have to let him be rough with me—whether that was in the bed or by going upside my head, depending on his mood. I knew he had a problem. Well, by extension and affiliation, WE had a problem and I could not fix it. I packed up, determined to get to a place of peace where I could love me. It turns out that I found that 8,588 miles away from where I was born.

## Reconciliation in South Africa

The School for International Training (SIT) has an amazing study abroad program that I was blessed to participate in. I initially wanted to go to Spain to reinforce my Spanish skills, but decided that I needed to become fluent in my culture before studying the culture of others (yet again). It's quite interesting that when I initially told people I was going to Spain, their response was, "Oh it's going to be so beautiful there." However, when I revealed that I was going to South Africa instead, the response was very different, filled with doubt and fear and rooted in sheer ignorance. People advised, "Be careful" as if it were uncivilized when the truth was our disconnection to the African continent is what was really uncivilized.

When flight day came, I said goodbye to my friends and got good and drunk for the 18-hour flight back to the roots I had never seen. I didn't want to sit with the group. I had been shocked to see only two other Black students in the group of 22. I just knew more Black students would be on this trip to the motherland; however, much like I would discover when I arrived, white people were very interested in Africa.

I wanted to sleep as much as I could, but I ended up writing for most of the trip. I was in economy, but once I got a glimpse of first class I knew I had to be there instead. I needed a first-class experience to complement my international exposure. I was determined to make it to first class so I waited until the lights went out during the night portion and slipped into an open seat. I didn't tiptoe though; I walked boldly and confidently as if I belonged there and I felt like I did.

To my surprise, the seats let all the way back, turning into a bed. Instead of paper napkins, they had real cloth towels. Even the meals were better. I sat there thinking about all the things I'd been told about money, including "money doesn't grow on trees." Well, wherever it grew, I needed to be there. I began to see that money isn't evil; it's a tool.

I got to be in first class for five hours before I saw the flight attendants whispering, looking and pointing. We had already made our layover in Dakar so I knew they couldn't kick me off the flight. The next stop was mine anyway, but I didn't want no smoke at that altitude. I still had a tendency to go off a little, or a lot depending on the day, so I decided I would just go back to regular class before they had a chance to out me. I thought about my favorite unbothered rebuttal, "I been kicked out of better places." I laughed to myself thinking this time it is indeed a better place. In fact, it's the best place so I better not mess around and get kicked out of the motherland before I even arrive!

When I got there, I felt like Nas and Keisha at the end of *Belly*. The grass sure was a different color green and the sky a different color blue. Some things stayed the same though. The first day in Johannesburg, I already knew that I was going to have a tough time keeping quiet. From the very start, the ugliest of elitism and privilege reared its head. Some of the students would make culturally insensitive comments or act like they were in the wild. One day I had enough, and with one question they stopped and knew I wasn't the one to play with. I simply said, "Have you read about the history of cavemen that lived so barbarically that they inflicted indescribable torture on people and sometimes resorted to cannibalism?"

The only Black male professor, Dr. Twali, heard me and smirked, later referring to me as a young Angela Davis. You could have knocked me over with a feather. I'd admired her since I first read a book of poems by her and Nikki Giovanni in the University of Illinois library at the age of 12 when my mother worked there. Him calling me that only made me even less hesitant to speak up when they spoke out. Although the program encouraged healthy dialog, I knew that I'd become labeled as the group's rabble-rouser. At first I was bashful about that and tried to just be quiet and enjoy the experience, but I couldn't and I didn't. I embraced my ability to speak out truthfully and unapologetically even in a room filled with whiteness. I did it respectfully and professionally, but I wasn't gonna be forced to be quiet. If there was anywhere worth speaking out, it had to be in Africa.

I had brought far too much luggage. I had three suitcases and everything of value I owned. I feared that it wouldn't be there when I got back "home" if I left it so I took it all with me. This wasn't the first international experience for many of my counterparts and they seemed to know that it was a backpack kinda trip. But here I was lugging around a whole bunch of baggage, both literally and figuratively, including a Louis Vuitton purse that my Momma won as a birthday gift for me while gambling on the casino boat. Once we made it from Joburg to our principal location in Durban, I knew it was time to lighten my load—in more ways than one.

**The Workshop in Durban, South Africa. Transportation center, mall and economic hub for street vendors.**

I was on a quest to learn about me and to fall in love with me ... all of me. Our journey started with a six-week homestay with a native South African family. I specifically requested a Black South African Family. The father had recently passed away and they played Luther Vandross's "Dance With My Father" almost every night. The house was nice and had a pool in the backyard.

**Backyard swimming at my homestay family's residence in Durban, South Africa**

They even had a housekeeper or domestic worker as they called it. The first time she came to pick up my laundry, I told her I could wash my own clothes. She said, "It's no problem," and I insisted that she let me do it myself until she handed me the washboard and said, "Do you need me to make the laundry water in the tub?" I said, "Yes please because I need to at least wash my underwear. A respectable woman can at least do that." She laughed and together we washed my clothes the old-fashioned way. She said, "You have rich lady clothes." I responded with a smile, "Nope, I know how to shop well. My Mother taught me how to find a deal and look like a million dollars on a budget." I decided to give her and my homestay sisters some Levi shorts and pants I got on sale. You would have thought I told them they won the lotto!

I honestly didn't know about Afrikaners until I started researching South Africa to prepare for the journey. The more I learned about apartheid, the more I saw similarities to the system being combatted by the Civil Rights Movement. I've always loved people who showed me love regardless of color. God's word tells me to love ALL people, but I have to admit learning about so many atrocities and violations to basic human rights both in the United States and in South Africa (and many other countries) made me apprehensive to say the least.

**Taken on: Table Mountain in Cape Town, South Africa**

At first I didn't speak much so I could blend and listen in. The natives saw me as Zulu as long as I didn't speak. As soon as I spoke a couple words though, they'd say with widened eyes, "Oh you're from America!" One fellow told me, "That's where the roads are paved in gold." (If there were roads paved in gold in the United States, I had never seen them, but there was certainly gold in Africa. The ironic part was other countries usually mined and claimed it.) I told him I grew up in an American ghetto which was much nicer than their poor neighborhoods but it nevertheless was the United States version of their shantytowns. I told him I was there on scholarship and most times couldn't afford to eat at restaurants before counting the exchange rate and checking my balance.

Me and Ebb (one of the only other black students, my girl Ebb from Spelman) cooked more than any of the other students. She was perfect at keeping me on point too, even though she was sometimes too bossy for me. That girl was ALWAYS on time and I was late every time. I tried to be more timely, but I dared one of our counterparts to even look like they wanted to make a CP time joke. I stayed ready like I had just read *Roots* and watched *Malcolm X*. Like Ebb didn't play about time, neither of us played about cultural sensitivity and respect. We were a minority in the group of students, yet majorly connected to the country so much so that natives often greeted us calling us "Sis" and saying "Welcome Home." It was not the first time I have felt more at home somewhere else than I did at home on the streets of the southside of Chicago, but at the same time it reminded me of all the amazing facets of where I come from. Oddly enough, it took going extremely far away from home to reconnect me to the parts of me and the parts of home that made me ... me.

I stopped taking the student buses and public transportation and started taking the minibus, known to locals as the Kombi. It was like the RideSharing Pool of South Africa. Yep, in Chicago and South Africa, we had ridesharing first, but in those days, there was no app for that or smart phones to put it on! As with many things, we had the innovative ideas, but were ahead of the technology curve.

Once I got more comfortable, I started to have conversations on the Kombi. I was learning just as much on the bus with the natives as I was at the University of KwaZulu Natal. Most times they wanted to know about America. Although I didn't mind sharing, I often had to remind them that I'd been displaced from my roots so rather than talk about the place where I'd been forced to assimilate, I wanted to unlearn some things and educate myself on the truth.

I knew just by getting off that plane that we had not been told the truth. I learned some harsh realities living and studying in post-apartheid South Africa. I arrived during the 10-year celebration of the ending of apartheid. I kept thinking just 10 years ago there was apartheid, and just 50 years ago the Civil Rights Movement happened and there were sundown towns in parts of the United States. Actually, there are still sundown towns in the United States! In addition, within the last three years we've seen the tragic deaths and travesties of justice of Breonna Taylor, George Floyd, Ahmaud Arbery and so many others who deserve to have their names mentioned. I want to say all of their names, even the ones we don't know about, but there are too many to list (more on this in the "Overcoming Injustice" chapter).

One night I missed the Kombi and had to take a cab home. I knew that he'd be taking the long route there just based on my accent and his excitement when he clicked the fare box that looked like something out of a western movie. I thought, "Well, if I'm gonna pay extra, I need to include this in my research." I started off subtly, asking him about South African food. Food is always a way to bridge gaps because no matter what color or language, in order to live we all need to eat. (Shout out to Live In The Content Kitchen™!) After we talked about how I didn't like fufu and fish soup, I slid into more pressing issues that I had long wanted to know. I took a deep breath and asked, "Do native Africans dislike African-Americans? I mean I know some that marry African-American women, but it is rumored that native Africans really don't like us. What are your thoughts?" He took the same labored deep breath I took to ask the question before he went on with his answer. With a thick accent, he said, "We will play and have fun with American women or even marry to become citizens but many of us don't take you serious. The problem is Black Americans don't always try to embrace their identity. They have been removed from their culture and don't seek to return. Even in America, the land of milk and honey, we think sometimes some of you are lazy." His words stung but I appreciated his honesty. Like he had dropped the mic, we pulled up to my homestay. I tipped him and hopped out, confused about how what he had said made me feel. Not long after though, I would attain further education as to the effects of socioeconomic racism in South Africa.

At home, I was an Urban Studies and Public Policy major, a first-hand witness of gentrification on the southside of Chicago and a student on a campus in New Orleans that was once a plantation. Studying this area led me to think about issues such as hearing that low-income housing was placed near Lake Michigan as a buffer since it was believed it would someday overflow. (In time, I would realize I am that overflow and abundance.) Issues of racial segregation as a result of socioeconomic segregation would also become a huge topic of discussion.

With my background, quite naturally, I chose to study post-apartheid spatial development and low-income housing provision while overseas. I'd recently studied the Chicago Housing Authority's Plan for Transformation, and I wanted to examine the similarities of what I'd previously come to identify as redlining and what occurred in South Africa with the Zulus and other native African people. I wanted to go beyond what I read and do field experience so I went to the bank to inquire about the process of getting a home loan. While I waited in the lobby to speak with a representative, I imagined that I was actually coming to buy a building in South Africa that would house children from Chicago when they came to tour the motherland. I envisioned it having an ice-cream shop at the bottom with a picture of my late grandfather, "The Singing Ice Cream Man." My big dream came to an abrupt stop when I heard the bank teller call my name.

No one that I'd seen thus far were female or "colored" so when I saw this brown woman in the position of personal banker I let out a sigh of relief. That relief was short-lived. I had been practicing my Zulu by collecting marketing materials in the native language and translating them to English so I asked, "Do you have any marketing materials in Zulu?" The next thing that happened still bothers me to this day. She laughed, not smirked, but outright laughed and replied, "Why would we have brochures in Zulu?" Confused I said, "Because it's the language of the native people." To my surprise and utter disbelief, she responded matter-of-factly, "But they are not the ones with the money. The brochures are only offered in the language spoken by Afrikaners." My response to that is a book in itself. What I will say now is Africa like the United States is the real-life version of *The Haves and the Have Nots*.

**Welcoming celebration from village tribal dancers in Soweto**

When we left our family homestay visits with both a Zulu South African family and a Colored South African family, it was time for a two-week homestay in rural Soweto (South West Townships), a poor town with unpaved roads and no running water. The moment we got off the bus, I felt sad for being there to "study" the struggle that people had learned to live and thrive in. I couldn't justify the need to "tour" their plight without contributing to the improvement of their situation. So when the young man who had become my walking companion asked, "Can you leave me with something?" I gave what little I had on me, even though for us it was pocket change. Suddenly twenty children encircled me, some prying at my fistful of change. I felt so naive as the tour leaders made their way to "rescue" me, but I also felt moved to do something meaningful while I was in the country. For that reason, I was happy to learn that the program I was in with the School for International Training did contribute monetarily to each family that allowed us to stay, and the tours were paid for so we were contributing to the local economy.

My colleague joked about me being a tough city girl, but I was mortified by the idea of going to an outhouse at night. We'd only gone to Uncle Joe's in the daytime and even then we didn't drink anything in the hours before we arrived and/or used the bathroom at a gas station about a mile from Uncle Joe's shack before our visits. Grandma made sure we stopped at the fillin' station, as she called it. The thought of something literally biting me in the butt was enough for me to avoid the outhouse as much as possible. In reality though, I was not prepared for the true depths of the poverty we were about to encounter.

Although I managed to keep out of the outhouse, nights were still rough because the mice played on the tin roof and that concerned me too. I've always had a fear of rodents, but we always had a cat so that never became an issue. There I was scared by night and adventurous by day. The resiliency of the people was shown as they walked a mile both ways to access clean water and then harvested food for dinner. I had my first lessons in farming in Soweto where I learned to till the land and plant seeds while gathering vegetables for dinner. Everything was based on timing and order. When you have to live minimally, you learn how necessary it is to pivot in order.

Those two weeks in Soweto, I got to hear stories, and share in cultural connections and exotic experiences. While some people considered where I grew up to be pretty rough, we never had to overcome the challenges that Soweto residents pressed through with pride on a daily. What this encounter highlighted is while I can talk about the richness of the land, culture and people, despite the wealth of Africa, the gold is still disproportionately in the hands of the people who colonized it.

We left Soweto at the end of our stay, and a local burger joint was our very first stop before we split to our independent homestays. When we were done with all the family homestay parts of our trip, we had an independent study portion that allowed us to choose where we wanted to live for the last six weeks of the program. I chose a beachfront midrise on the lakefront (years later the building made it to the background of a Ludacris video called "Pimpin' All Over The World"). I had three roommates in a two-bedroom, but we were living in luxury because the house wasn't small and we could stand on our balcony to breathe in the water and feel the breeze. Around that time, I remember trying to get my absentee ballot in for John Kerry who was running against George W. Bush. Bush's campaign promo had a black background with his face looking stoic with a W in the middle. It looked very much like the advertisement for an anarchist or dictator. I ended up burning one of those posters on our balcony. I wasn't a fan of Bush, but I didn't know that even he could be trumped.

Ebb chose a quiet, residential area in one of the more affluent communities where she lived with two other students. It was a cute little cottage with Victorian-style windows around the kitchen. I had spent the night after one of our nights out in Durban and when I got up in the morning to make breakfast, a monkey came in the window and took a banana! I'm pretty sure I remember this relative of Curious George jumping back on the tree closest to the window and looking back at us while eating the banana. Truth is definitely stranger than fiction!

When Thanksgiving rolled around, I knew me and Ebb had to save dinner. We brought Atlanta and Arkansas (by way of Chicago) right there to my kitchen off the beach. I brought my Granny's "down south" peach cobbler recipe from the southside of Chicago to South Africa and it was a hit. I had burned it when I first made it because I didn't realize the degrees were in Celsius rather than Fahrenheit, but this time I got it just right. We didn't want to be too cliché so we made fried and baked chicken.

Between bites, we talked about applying to law school. My girl Ebb was also there helping me cook. I shared how I initially wanted to attend Howard University Law School, but was dissuaded from doing so by a professor at an international symposium. The reasoning he gave was attending an HBCU for both undergraduate and law school would be a red flag for employers that I lacked diversity or rather exposure to diverse environments. Ultimately, it didn't matter if two HBCUs was a red flag to white firms. At the time though, I didn't know that they didn't deserve me anyway.

After asking me what HBCU stood for, Amy, my Caucasian colleague, said it was surprising that I even had to consider something like that. She said, with a slightly nervous laugh, "I just pick the best school and they send my Daddy the bill." I didn't laugh because after my scholarships were used up, that bill was coming to me by way of Sallie Mae and it was sure to come like the midnight train to Georgia. That Sallie Mae student loan demon will probably be part of my forthcoming *Ted Talk* I'm speaking into existence. I didn't know back then that I didn't want to give a big firm that much power over me. And I sure didn't want to attend a predominantly white institution (PWI) in order to qualify to work 60-hour weeks to build someone else's dream for a small fraction of the profit. I had worked 60 hours a week as a manager in corporate America and I knew as a mother I didn't want that. I wanted financial freedom and flexibility. I just didn't yet have a complete idea of how to obtain it.

At the time though, I thought if I have to go to a PWI after graduation, let me at least immerse myself in the culture in South Africa as much as possible.

All was going well at dinner until one of our colleagues was sitting at the breakfast bar talking and she dipped her spoon in the entire pan of peach cobbler. I gave Ebb the "I'm about to set it off look" and she just shook her head. I thought maybe she won't dip it back in or maybe it was a clean spoon and she just wanted one taste. Two double dips later, I couldn't take no mo'. I knew it would come out a little rough, but I didn't care. She was gonna learn today. I grabbed a bowl and said, "You can't sit here and eat from the whole pan like that. Let me scoop this part you've eaten off of into a bowl for you." She immediately decided that she'd had enough peach cobbler for the evening and it was time for her to go. She didn't appreciate being checked and thought we'd ask her to stay. Nope, the party was over for her and I made sure she saw me throw away that lil' square she was eating from. And no, there was no to go plate for her! It was just time for her to go!

South Africa gave me such a rich landscape of memories. It connected me to my roots and showered me with the love I didn't realize I had been missing. The country embraced me and it would stay with me forever.

## Connection Clue

How have you been forced to affirm yourself even when society invalidates you? You are the first to know your thoughts. What you think of yourself matters. How you talk to yourself matters. Let me make it crystal clear: YOU MATTER, NO MATTER WHAT THEY SAY. You matter, even when they don't say you do. Be kind to yourself. The world won't always embrace you. In fact, most times we will have to stand strong and firm in the face of formidable opponents and longstanding systems meant for our demise. Arrogance is not the same as confidence. We can be proud, yet humble. Jesse Jackson's mantra "keep hope alive" translated to me as "keep hope from dying." Sometimes hope barely has a pulse. You might fall low, but do not faint in welldoing. God sees you and He sees the best in you. You are the apple of His eye and His greatest creation. We are descendants of royalty and have an inheritance.

**Audacity Affirmation**

I will stay hopeful by being a beacon of light that shines in dark places. Even when it's not a popular thing to do, I will stand up for what is right and righteous, armed with the breastplate of truth as my primary weapon against the hands of the enemy. I will advocate for change, advocate for the disadvantaged, and be a voice for the voiceless. In a small step or a large leap, I will help to create the change we all need to see.

# Chapter 5

## Deferred Dreams & Wooden Nickels

And we know that all things work together for good to them that love God, to them who are the called according to his purpose.
Romans 8:28

Even before going overseas, I was no stranger to the problems that existed as a result of overcrowded and impoverished communities. I had witnessed large tour buses filled with gawking eyes accessing and assessing the value of my soon-to-be gentrified community, value which did not include me. Therefore, I could easily relate to many of the natives I encountered, with their stories of injustice, tragedies and yet still triumphs. I had volunteered with local non-governmental agencies working to develop communities and provide shelter to orphan children, but I still wanted to do more than my semester abroad would allow. I had no idea of the massive calamity I would experience closer to home when I returned to the city that I'd come to know as my second home. It would indeed show that there were conditions at home that needed to change in a massive way.

I returned to New Orleans the following fall to begin my senior year. My excitement quickly dwindled as I soon realized that this hurricane season would be different from previous ones. Not only was the university closing, the entire city was called to evacuate. It was extremely overwhelming and devastating to see familiar areas submerged. The chaos was compounded when I was forced to quickly rearrange my educational plans. It was important to me that I did not take the semester off and that I return to New Orleans to be a part of rebuilding my home institution and the City of New Orleans.

The Hilton New Orleans became our new campus, where we lived and attended classes. Working simultaneously as a full-time overnight cashier at a downtown parking facility did not stop me from what I believed to be my true mission in returning to New Orleans. I helped to organize and participated in monthly cleanup initiatives in surrounding communities, some of which I had become familiar with as an intern for the Housing Authority of New Orleans. As a student organizer, I spoke with people who told me horrific stories, expressing their concerns. Many conversations concluded with the same type of questioning, "Is this fair? Is this even legal? What are my rights?" I became a referral representative for many, trying to locate resources for those most in need.

My experiences showed me how the law is relative in so many aspects of our society. While being a lawyer in general is advocating for the interests and rights of others, public interest law began to stand out as something worth pursuing. I saw this type of work as being synonymous with being on the ground post-Katrina. It seems to be the sector of law that is most in touch with the people since it involves homelessness, deportation and child neglect, all of which are high stakes issues clients may be facing.

As I reflect on my life experiences, it seems as if I have always been in preparation to be an advocate. My Grandmother who was very active in my raising always told me in her Southern accent, "Don't take no wooden nickels." I started refusing wooden nickels early on when in grammar school I challenged my pending suspension for finally standing up to the school bully after repeatedly informing faculty of his antics. In high school, I voluntarily met with school officials to dispute a rule requiring students to attain a minimum score on a standardized test as a prerequisite to enrolling in AP classes and earned a 3.9 GPA resulting in an amendment to that rule. These lessons taught me the art of reasoning and negotiation at an early age. They also prepared me to challenge what is said to me, not simply accept it as right just because someone says so. This is especially true if that which is said is with the intent of underestimating or limiting your trajectory.

In the hallway of my housing complex, I once encountered a young boy who said to me, "What you always studying for?" I proudly responded, "I'm going to be a lawyer one day." He said, "You should be a secretary; you don't look like no lawyer." I asked him what a lawyer looked like and he responded with "a white man." As a child, his comment crushed me, but now I am determined to expand the limits of what people feel is possible.

I am Black. I am a woman. I am an unwed mother. I am from the ghetto. I have experienced poverty and benefited from welfare. I've learned that one person's pocket change doesn't actually change much, but mighty are the collective efforts of people who refuse to take wooden nickels and fight relentlessly to achieve positive change. All of my experiences have made me uniquely qualified to present perspective and sustainable solutions to those without a voice who would most likely fall victim to a broken system.

## Dream Deferred (The Greatest Inspiration)

During times of great transition, we often have other life-changing events in the midst. When I found out I was pregnant, I was interviewing for a managerial role at a car rental company at one of the busiest airports. As I was the only Black woman manager and the youngest manager I had to play a "game" just to maintain on so many levels.

I quickly discovered a hint of what I, in my pre-law school mind, thought could be labor law violations, so I started clocking in on the timeclock like unsalaried employees. Management quickly pulled me to the side and asked why. I replied, "Because managers work 10 hours a day, sometimes six days a week, but the schedule doesn't reflect that and neither does the hourly breakdown of our salary on the check stubs." After the white man took a pause, the Black manager said, "But Andrea you get a company car that makes up for the 10 hours that aren't reflected because they cover gas and insurance." Without hesitation, I turned and looked from him to the white manager and said, "Well if that's the case, then give me the option to turn in my car, give me the money and I'll drive my own car." The white manager was turning red and the Black manager had a look of concern like he was thinking "Yo' revolutionary, ungrateful ass gon' make the bosses mad!" He finally said, "Andrea, the company car is not an option; it comes with it. Think of it as a privilege that we give you a car with gas and insurance, saving you money." I thought, "A privilege to work 10 hours a week without compensation."

I walked out of the office because I knew it was a losing battle. I knew I was right, but like Granny used to say, "I didn't have no win," or so I thought at the time. As it turns out, my pre-law mind was correct about the company being law(less) and (out of) order. A few months after I ruffled feathers about tracking my time, I received an invitation to join a class-action lawsuit. Apparently, a few good men in New York had filed a case a year before for the same thing that I suspected was a violation of Fair Labor laws. I took it as another sign. I was already lawyering!

Just as I walked out of that meeting, I felt my baby's feet for the first time. I thought I would feel his little kicks when we woke up for tea before work in the morning, but no they came at work when I was storming out of the office heated. I looked up from my stomach and saw nothing but snow and rows and rows of cars that I had to have scanned for an inventory audit. For a quick moment, I thought back to when I'd go to park the ice-cream truck with my Paw Paw as a kid. There were rows and rows of Good Humor ice-cream trucks, and he owned a handful. Briefly I thought about how I could franchise a car rental company of my own. I'd been in the industry for years and some of my college colleagues had gone the same route. I quickly dismissed the thought. I was daydreaming, but reality set in. I was a pregnant manager and needed to figure out how I could get FMLA to have maternity leave time.

Those thoughts about my college colleagues led me to call Ena. I didn't get an answer so I eventually left a message on her Mom's phone line. When her Mother called me back, it was to deliver some heartbreaking news. My friend Ena had been killed in a car crash. Even as I was preparing to bring a life into the world, a friend I had shared such a pivotal time with in college had passed on. It took me a while to get myself together.

When I could think straight again, I reflected on how I'd graduated from counting boxes at UPS to counting cars, and still I was unfulfilled in the corporate mill. Me and my curly fro just weren't a good fit. (I only wore it straight during the interview. Weren't they in for a surprise!) I knew I was still going to go to law school with my baby. It was just temporary to get me over to the next blessing.

I got mad the day before when one of the men I managed said, "If that was my baby, you'd be home with your feet up. Why you still working? I can be your baby's stepdaddy." He must have had a second job I didn't know about because he didn't make enough to keep himself at home. I contemplated writing him up for that stepdaddy remark, but I didn't want to be the cause of trouble for a working Black man.

After my FMLA ran out, I got an internship with the Department of Transportation in Boston. I wasn't at home to feel any embarrassment so I went on Commonwealth Avenue with a tin can in a Notre Dame shirt asking people to help me get to law school. I don't know how I thought asking for change would add up to $60k to pay for even just my first year, but I felt God telling me to humble myself and do it as if I was proving how much I really wanted it. After two weeks of going out there, I had gotten to know the panhandlers and there was one that had more sense than met the eye.

This man was wise and looked out for me. He shared that they took shifts in the hot spots so there wouldn't be more than one person asking for change at the same location. He also gave me his shift when I got off work on Fridays because it was busier and drunks are generous. It is somehow crazy to say it, but there was a whole system for settling … After I told him about my whole law school saga, he mentioned that there was a man I needed to meet. He said that this man "talked smooth and intellectual," but was still down for the people and relatable, just like me. He gave me Mr. King's information and told me to tell him that he referred me so that he would see me right away. He held true to his word.

I had prepared some questions and wanted to tell Mr. King about my law school dilemma. Before I had the chance to bring that up, he told me that I asked the right questions and asked if I'd considered being a TV show host or a journalist. I told him that I liked writing but not that much and I didn't really see myself being on camera but that I "wanted to use my voice to advocate for the voiceless and shed light in dark places." He laughed and asked if I had just made that up on the fly. I admitted with a smile that I had. Mr. King said, "In that case, maybe you need to be a politician." I replied, "Well, my chance to be great lies in me finding a way to go to Notre Dame this fall." Mr. King's smirk disappeared and with a stern face he looked me in the eye like he knew me my whole life and said, "My Dear, you're giving them far too much weight. The school doesn't make you.

You were born great and the legacy of Notre Dame had nothing to do with that. That, young lady, is the legacy of your ancestors' hopes and dreams."

I felt like Maya Angelou had freed the caged bird herself in that moment. I didn't know what I was supposed to do, but for the first time I entertained the notion I could do it in excellence even if I didn't graduate from Notre Dame. I thought God was gonna use this connection to lead to a check, but instead it opened the door to what could be. His words were a spark I would need later when the embers of my dreams seemed to go out.

I returned to Chicago to re-evaluate and plan my next move. My son's father had come a long way from the boy I knew when we were kids. He had money and he "took care of me," but I didn't know where that money was coming from so I wasn't banking on it. I worked up until that last day and had my son on my day off at the best hospital in the city, a feat in and of itself. Once I'd managed that with the grace of God, I had to tackle getting him to be a patient at the University. Despite my rocky relationship with the historically exclusive (now trying to be inclusive) institution, I learned one thing about a particular doctor that had me sold. He was the pediatrician of Sasha and Malia Obama ... Yep, it was the Obama doctor for me! One way or the other, by any means necessary, I prayed that God would manage that waitlist. Good insurance got me on the list, but God enforced the policy! Won't He do it!

Having my son was the scariest, most faithful, and most love-filled experience of my life. My baby didn't cry at first. They didn't put him on my chest. I tried to get up and walk over to him and almost fell down. In that moment, waiting on him to cry, I cried and prayed. Then I heard him and cried more. Looking at him was like love made sense for the first time ever. His Dad was there, but he was sleeping most of the time. It was just me and my baby. I tried to wake my son's Dad up, but he was so mean I started to prefer when he was asleep. The nurse that kind of became my hospital auntie said jokingly, "Let that man sleep. At least he's here with you." I smirked and thought to myself, "Yeah, at least, 'cause it could be worse." I wanted more, but I was repeatedly confronted by the mindset of "at least" while wondering when does more, most, and best come into play.

I remember trying to balance going back to work, breastfeeding, applying for legal internships and scholarships all the while trying to keep a man who was seemingly never satisfied happy. I could deal with the rest of the things, but that last thing was starting to make me feel so incomplete. My life started to revolve around how he felt and what I could do to make him happy so he wouldn't be so mean to me. Lawd, we were turning into my Mom and Dad right before my eyes! I often felt like I was falling apart, but I held on to my dream, even when my grip started to slip. I didn't start to feel like myself until just around my son's first birthday, which is also around the time that I was robbed at gunpoint.

The end of the summer came and went and none of my efforts amassed enough for me to foot the bill so essentially Notre Dame gave me the boot. I went back to work in management that fall. It was my first day as a manager, and I had a company car again, so I should've been happy. I was at first, especially considering how difficult things had gotten from exhausting all my resources trying to secure financial aid and relocate to attend law school. I had to go through yet another application season, but in the meantime that job was a means to provide for my son. So I decided I would be happy that while I still felt lost and out of alignment, God was still providing.

I gave myself a good pep talk in the bathroom of Midway Airport and walked out ready. Just as I hit the corner to go to the sales counter, I saw a huge sea of Notre Dame logos and branded apparel. There were literally hundreds of fans jam-packed in the lobby to rent cars. I looked out in utter shock. I felt like the devil was winning. Where was the lesson in this to have it thrown in my face right after I had prayed so hard to just be grateful and try to be happy? I had to go back to the bathroom to gather myself. After several splashes of water to my face, I prayed that God would keep me faithful in His process even in uncertain moments, amidst doubt and against any fear. I prayed that He would fortify me for the journey. I had to come back to that bathroom three more times to pep talk myself through the day.

In that moment, I was managing everything but my racing thoughts kept repeating that everything I'd done was in vain because even with the GoFundMe I created I just couldn't make it to Notre Dame. And then a customer said, "I know you love Notre Dame; everybody loves Notre Dame." I couldn't hold it in. I said, "I guess I had a love for Notre Dame, but not anymore." I told my accepted but couldn't afford to go story, the abridged version. The man felt so sad for me that he told me to keep hope alive and gave me a $50 tip when I handed him his rental agreement. I said, "Thank you," but smirked at the fact that he had used a Jesse Jackson coined phrase. Yes, I had even gone to PUSH asking for help to keep my dream alive, but when push came to shove, even Jesse Jackson couldn't help me. Mmmm hmmm, I was mad at Jesse too! I was mad at myself and I was mad as hell at Sallie Mae.

After that, I had to go to the bathroom and cry and pray some more. This time I felt like asking God, "Was it all for nothing? Why would I chase it so hard only to still fall short?" I hoped maybe one day God would use me as a vehicle to create funding sources for students like me to have greater access and support to attend top law schools and graduate with less undergraduate debt. I wanted there to be purpose in my struggle and to make an impact and leave more equitable opportunities for those coming behind me.

Still doggedly determined, I was pursuing my dream of going to a top law school while trying to get a scholarship for my son to attend his first school. After waiting on the waitlist for preschool programs for quite a while, I asked the school for help. The lady told me she'd give me until the end of summer—a month after the deadline—like the money would magically appear. Estoppel after estoppel appeared, but I was determined not to stop.

While working, I planned to apply the next year even more strategically. At the beginning of my shift, I pulled the list of business account rentals, paying particular attention to the law firms that had employees renting vehicles. I researched firms and familiarized myself with the practice areas of the most frequent renters in an attempt to figure out what area of law I wanted to practice. One day I walked in late from rushing to get my son to school on time and went to the front counter to check in with the agents. I was the only manager that worked the counter with agents. I also had less customer complaints during my shifts. I noticed a gentleman looking for a Tahoe XL, but we only had smaller trucks available. He explained that he was going on a skiing trip with family and needed the room and the rack for equipment. I couldn't get a large truck from another location so I mapped out a location on his route that had one and sent him there in the car we had so he could switch into a larger vehicle before picking up the equipment in the next town. He was so grateful and complimented my effort and service.

It wasn't until I printed out the rental agreement that I realized he was an attorney at one of the biggest firms in the city so of course I had to tell him about my law school quest. He thanked me for helping him and gave me his business card. He said, "I'd be more than happy to help however I can. Just reach out and I can connect you with someone at the firm in the area of law you're interested in." I reached out the following week to make sure that he had a seamless experience after leaving the airport. I also mentioned that I was applying for school again and asked if he could let me know of any funding scholarships or contacts at the school. To my surprise, he responded and said he'd like to provide me with a letter of recommendation to support my application. Although I had three letters of recommendation already, I knew having one from a lawyer at a top firm would only further enhance my application. I was so grateful because for the first time since not being able to attend, I really felt that God still had His hand on the situation if only I could pivot and persist.

I was preparing to quit my job over the next four to five months to move to whichever school gave me the best opportunities. I spent my lunch breaks searching the internet for scholarships and completing applications. I had told my son's father that I would go to school in the Midwest, but since my Notre Dame nightmare and our relationship downward spiral I decided to go to the best place, which meant the best schools for my son and the most scholarship money for me. I applied to five schools and because I thought the rankings mattered so much, three of them were schools in the upward tier like Notre Dame. I later realized that the ranking was not as based on the quality of education as much as I'd believed. Indeed, the ranking system was actually more biased than I thought.

During those months, I gave a lot of thought to what one of my more conservation mentors had said, in essence that an Ivy League school was my ticket to success and if I was fortunate enough to be admitted I simply needed to find a way to make attending a reality. While I knew that she had more experience, more insight, and more money than me, I also knew that she was speaking from a place of privilege. She simply couldn't fathom money being a barrier to me attending an Ivy League institution.

It took me a while to confidently declare that I was my own ticket to success. It wasn't the school, the job, the titles, nor licenses and certificates that would determine my success, but rather my resilience and faith under fire that would keep me consistently overcoming anything that was thrown my way. However, before this realization became part of my framework, I was fixed on the idea that I had to get to law school by any means necessary.

I decided to go to the church. The story of my life as a parishioner was asking for money to help pay tuition. I didn't want to ask again, but I had to. I dropped off my son to my Grandma and went to the 24-hour copy and print shop and created a 15-page proposal that included my bio, grades, acceptance letters, letters of recommendation and cost of attendance. I left the print shop at 6 am the next morning with a bound, polished proposal in hand. Before I pulled off, I looked down at my phone to a text saying, "You need to come and get your son instead of laying up all night like you don't have any real responsibilities." I decided that I didn't have the energy to convince nor explain because our next move would get us away from all the negative talk anyway.

I thought about transferring my job to the state where I would be attending law school, but quickly realized that working and attending school like I did in undergraduate school wasn't going to work at that level as a single mom. As much as I didn't want to give up the company car and the benefits, I knew I had to resign. I was prepared to submit my letter of resignation, but the same week a car pulled out in front of me and hit me as I was coming across a light. Despite the accident not being my fault, the company still decided to let me go. The odd thing is that when I went to the company meeting, their tone was kind of like, "Well, we know that you wanted to go to law school anyway so we wish you success, but we're going to go ahead and part ways." Really though, I didn't feel the least bit sad. I considered it a ghetto blessing. Instead of getting fired and leaving with nothing, I could file for unemployment benefits. One way or another ... won't He do it!

But let me tell you what happened when they put up a fight regarding my unemployment benefits. Instead of just granting the unemployment, a team of mean male managers decided to challenge it. The letter informing me that it was being contested came in the mail right after I had left for Portland. I just happened to answer an unknown number on my way to orientation. The judge informed me that I had a scheduled arbitration. I had never received unemployment and didn't know what to expect but I said, "Okay, I'm ready." We went back and forth, point for point, and then it was time for my closing statement. I felt like Matthew McConaughey in *A Time To Kill*, which has one of the best closing statements I've seen beside Johnnie Cochran in the O.J. trial.

I had to make my point before a jury unlike my peers. I concluded with this: "Like most companies, their culture and practices are not based on what's best for employees, but rather what's best for the bottom line. They should not be allowed to operate in this way at my expense. Based on the evidence, it is my belief and understanding that the application of labor law policies would warrant me to be compensated unemployment for wrongful termination despite this being an at-will state." I didn't know if I was saying the right thing, but I said it and when I was done the Judge immediately said, "Wow! Have you been to law school?" I replied, "I actually start in a couple weeks and am preparing for orientation." He said, "Congratulations, you're going to do well. That was a great closing!" I let out a sigh of relief as I heard one of the managers breathe a sigh of defeat. He knew they were gonna have to shut up and pay out!

The closer I got to leaving Chicago, the more and more drama seemed to come my way. It seemed as if nobody understood me and everybody seemed to be coming at me crazy as hell. I had bet everything on going to Notre Dame, so much so that I'd gotten behind on my rent and was facing eviction court. I asked a relative for help—one that I had helped more times than many—and was told no. I was evicted a few months later. That same relative I asked to sublease my apartment while I went away to school went and applied for an apartment in the same building I was evicted from and had the audacity to call me and tell me that her application was denied. The cherry on the top was when she asked for my advice on how to reapply and get approved! I was decades younger than her and she saw fit to ask me for information to help her when she had the resources to help me and simply chose not to. I just got off the phone and shook my head.

I was sick and tired of most people. I had let people's ill intentions, gossip, doubt, and negative words fuel my desire to push for success. It took me a while to realize that negative energy couldn't sustain me at the next level. I had to redirect my energy to positive sources of motivation. I had to choose to take the upper road even when the pavement was rough. It's easy to clap back; it's harder to come back on the come up. I didn't want to delay my overcoming by addressing foolishness so I chose to endure the process on the way to the progress. I didn't care what it looked like and who believed the breakthrough wasn't coming. I kept building even if I looked like a fool to people without the vision to see the making of something great. Reflecting on my journey, I see great parallels to the story of Noah. He was asked to build an ark when at that time there had never been rain!

And I Daniel alone saw the vision: for the men that were with me saw not the vision; but a great quaking fell upon them, so that they fled to hide themselves.
Daniel 10:7

It was no longer my job to try to convince people. I was more interested in how God would use me to manifest a blessing using this very mess. So, even in the situations where I am accountable for the mess, in the mess, there is a message. Bashing them back when they did me wrong was not worth me diverting my energy from the magic God was making. It's okay if in the beginning only God and I see the tapestry. In His timing, it will all come together beautifully.

In the meantime, I couldn't find peace anywhere, not even at my Grandma's house. The breaking point came when a family fight happened in front of my son. I ended up spending the last three weeks of my time in Chicago in a deluxe suite at the Amber Inn, a 3-star hotel on the south side. Although I could have stayed on my aunt's discount, I didn't want her to know what I was going through and I couldn't afford an extended stay at a hotel downtown, even with the discount. Ironically, I was in the same suite that me and N'eres stayed in after prom a little over 10 years prior. One would think I'd hit rock bottom at that point, but I had sense enough to still look at the bright side, even if it was slightly and temporarily dim.

I'd gotten cool with the owner of the hotel, a sophisticated Black woman who blessed us with a refrigerator in our room and made sure that security looked out for my son and me. We were just blocks away from a grocery store with a hot food bar and grill. On top of that, we had so many Groupons for Chicago's Home of Chicken & Waffles down the street and ate there so much we got on a first name basis with a couple of the waitstaff.

Even though I only had to wait one more week before we left for law school, I was starting to get discouraged. God knows exactly when to throw you a sign of reassurance. My son and I would catch the church van home after services. I felt embarrassed that we were getting dropped off at The Amber Inn, but just as I started to think about having them drop us off at the grocery store down the street, the van made an abrupt stop at the Central Arms Hotel. The man blurted out, "Is this the right building? There's no address." The woman beside me shrunk down in her seat and quietly said, "This is it." If the Amber was a 3-star, Central Arms was definitely a no star filled with drug addicts, pimps and prostitutes. The woman didn't appear to have a substance abuse issue, but seemed to be going through a temporary shift similar to me. She clearly just wanted to get out and get it over with. I wanted to tell her that it was okay and not to be ashamed, but rather than make a scene, I just quietly said, "Have a blessed week" and I thanked God for our little room at The Amber.

> **"Love recognizes no barriers. It jumps hurdles, leaps fences, penetrates walls to arrive at its destination full of hope."**
>
> **—Maya Angelou**

The next week, we were prepared to hit the airport a day before my son's fifth birthday. We had a stop in Atlanta on the way to Portland. My Spelman buddy, Eb, that I'd studied abroad with in South Africa had recently left her management job at a rental car company to start a bakery business. She had taken the leap from corporate to full-time entrepreneurship and I was excited to support. She delivered a car-themed birthday cake right to the airport during our layover. My baby dug into the cake right there in the back seat of the car! Remembering how his little face lit up still brings joy to my heart. Seeing him excited about our new journey, I felt so confident that God was engineering a testimony. We were going to make it!

A week after we arrived in Portland, I'd moved to a dorm on the undergraduate campus. My son couldn't stay for long, but I wanted to give him a taste of the college experience at a young age. Luckily, my Grandmother was able to keep him for a couple of weeks while I got my housing situation together. Classes started and there was only one other Black girl in one of my classes and you could tell off the bat that she wasn't code switching but she was code stuck and straight from the suburbs, with very little understanding for the plight of the people. However, she was nice and pretty cool with me.

It only took a couple of weeks for her to find out that I was staying in the dorms. She excitedly said, "You can stay with me. I have a two bedroom." Although I was apprehensive, I was thankful. I nervously responded, "I'll have to bring my son with me. I'm flying back to Chicago to get him next week." She said, "Oh fun! You guys can have the second bedroom." I quickly asked if $400 a month would be enough. She said, "Sure, that's more than I expected."

I brought my son a bunch of transportation-themed toys from a couple of estate sales I went to: cars, trains, planes and antique boats. I only had an airbed and a toy chest in the room when I brought him back, but the room was decorated like a traveling adventure, from the map on the wall to the cartoon rug. I was grateful, but I had always had my own so I felt awkward. Our first night there, I watched him sleep and prayed that God would let us find a place in 90 days or less. I didn't have a lot of money and my credit was "so so" and so I really needed God to move on our behalf.

The next morning, I woke up on the floor surrounded by law books with my son snuggled up next to me. When I moved to get up, he moved too. I said, "Jeremiah, I don't want you sleeping on the floor. Why did you get out of the bed?" He said, "I want to lay with you Ma, even if it's on the floor. I just want to be by you." My heart melted. He was all the inspiration I needed. And he still is. That kind of love was enough to motivate me to work and pray to go from the floor to first class!

The campus shuttle we took to school went through neighboring Lake Oswego, an extremely wealthy neighborhood. One of the route stops was at a nice, gated complex that sat on a hill. I looked out of the window and said to myself, "I wish we could live here." Almost instantly, something told me to apply even though I just knew I couldn't get approved. Not only was my credit challenged, I had an eviction too. I had never asked anyone to cosign anything for me. In fact, I considered cosigning for someone to be a sin. Despite my reservations, I reached out to a mentor who had created a summer pre-law program I'd completed and explained my situation. Without hesitation, she agreed to cosign for the apartment! I went the next day and applied. A couple days later, I got the call that I was approved and didn't even need a consignor. To God be the glory!

Our new home was a two-bedroom, two-bathroom unit with a patio, marble countertops and stainless steel appliances. I'd had some nice apartments, but this was certainly the nicest and the most expensive. I was nervous signing a lease for $1,300 a month, but I was faithful that God would provide. He did and he had already made a way. He answered my prayer. I signed my lease on the 87th day.

I wasn't there for two whole weeks before I made acquaintance with my neighbors. The strangest one introduced herself before candidly asking me, "What made you move to Lake Oswego?" With no pause, she added, "You know they used to call it Lake No Negro, right?" I looked at her square in the eye and without hesitation responded, “Well, I wanted it to be at least one of us.”

My neighbor tried to get tight with me after making her “Lake No Negro” comment. It turns out her live-in boyfriend wasn’t always so nice to her and her grown son seemed to fight her from time to time. Often, she seemed like she just wanted to talk and needed a friend and since she was much more cautious about what and how she said things to me, I would sometimes sit on the porch and have wine with her while my son played with her dog.

One time she saw me coming in from an awards ceremony and she said, “Where are you coming from all dressed like you’re already a lawyer?” I replied, “Oh, an awards ceremony with an Oregon legal organization.” She said, “Oh, how was it?” Instead of me just saying fine and going on into the house, I had the audacity to hit her with the truth. Without pause, I said, “Well, I wish it were a little more diverse, but it is Portland so that seems to be a big ask.” With a disapproving look on her face, she asked, “Why does that matter to you so much? Does everything have to be about race, Andrea?” I let out a long sigh and contemplated just going inside because my feet were hurting, and I just wanted to take off my heels, but I decided to lay my burdens down right at her door before going in to have a nice cup of hot tea.

I got straight to the point and asked, “If you walked into an event and you were the only white person and everyone in the venue was black, would you then still be unclear as to why a lack of diversification is a problem?" She seemed perplexed and frustrated at this same time. I said, "I don't feel like doing this with you today" and finally went inside. I'm sure she is probably still trying to figure out why I always seemed so upset about race matters, but she didn't seem to realize she was living in the white privilege bubble. To her, I was just a disgruntled Black woman who was always complaining about discrimination and lack of representation. She definitely wasn't an ally and I had to put her in the PPWW (perpetually perplexed white woman) category.

So, Lake Oswego (now Lake One Negro) became home for me and my Black son. I heard it used to be a "sundown town" and here I was trying to learn legal lessons in a broken system to be a light in rooms that had long been darkened by white privilege. It was the first time I had lived in a racially homogenous state. If Portland was white, Lake Oswego was bleached, and to some my being there was a blemish. I resisted thoughts of inferiority and relentlessly persisted in my pursuit. I had a point to prove, not only to everyone else, but most importantly to myself and that began to fuel me even more.

I went to law school somewhat rosy-eyed and underestimating how inherently inhumane the law could be. It was so unfair how cases like the Central Park Five, now the Exonerated Five, still bring out so many fears for Black boys in Black mothers. What disturbed me most was the miscarriage of justice from the very beginning, specifically how mothers were misinformed and ill-advised about the rights of their minor sons. Fighting was something I'd become accustomed to, yet had grown tired of. Yet I still pursued the law because since becoming an avid *Law & Order* fan and seeing Lauren Lake appear on *The Ricki Lake Show*, I had wanted to be an attorney. So I had stepped out on faith and a few dollars with a baby and a dream. (Years later, I smiled when I realized my name even has dream in it!)

I arrived on campus without a clear plan, just like in undergrad, the difference being that I'd just turned 30 and had a son who wasn't even school-aged yet. I was determined to make it to law school and faithful that somehow God would make a way. After we got settled in Lake Oswego, classes were fully underway and I got a first-hand glimpse of some of the challenges that I would face going from a historically Black college to a PWI for the first time.

Often times when the law ran parallel with issues of race and social injustice, I'd find myself in the lecture halls feeling like Tupac's "All Eyes On Me." It was as if someone had silently said, "Let's see what the Black girl thinks." Early on, I did a disclaimer that basically said something to the effect that I was speaking from my perspective and it was not to be deemed as a representation of the collective experience. It was my attempt to give them a subtle warning to not hold all Black folks responsible if I happened to go off.

My favorite class was contracts, and my least favorite was civil procedure, but I'd later learn that perhaps it was indeed among the most important. The next most important was legal writing. My contracts professor had a way of breaking it down, and she used visuals so I was able to follow a little easier. Contracts class was one of the few classes I had to occasionally bring my son to. He'd sit on the steps of the lecture hall by my desk and color or do one of the worksheets I made for him. Most times he wanted to play a game on the phone instead, but he had things to occupy him so he kept quiet. Despite my attempts to minimize our presence, somehow we apparently still served as a distraction for one of the students who went to the professor asking if she'd have a talk with me about bringing my son to class because she wasn't able to focus on the lecture. When the professor told me I was irritated and relieved. I was irritated that someone had said that and relieved because they didn't say anything to me directly. I was too old and paying too much in Sallie's Mae's maze of debt to be getting kicked out of school!

I mused that it was probably one of the ones who smiled a nervous smile at me from time to time. Indeed, the professor moved five students on the assigned seating chart so I knew it must have been one of them. It was a bit surprising because all five of them were cordial and spoke to my son nicely. That just goes to show the "smilin' in your face," and then talk about you to the teacher behind your face folks are everywhere. Alexa, cue “Back Stabbers” by The O’Jays.

Fortunately for me and my son, the teacher had our backs, even behind our backs. She asked the snitch (I mean the student) to consider how I might feel and that maybe I didn’t have any other way to come to class without bringing my son. She went on to ask her to consider that maybe she should move her seat to accommodate her slight discomfort. I felt so thankful that the professor was able to deliver it in such a thought-provoking and kind way because I would have just said, “Why don’t you mind yo’ business and get out my face before you’re more than a little uncomfortable?”

Another challenging time during my time at law school was when a student made a statement that felt like he was intentionally trying to shock me to provoke a response. Charles casually said, “If you want to kill somebody with the least probability of severe consequences, kill a Black woman.” Before I could fix my mouth to reply, he tried to explain. He said under the law Black women are the least valued. Where the hell did he find that statistic?! I was already grappling with the statistic about the median net worth of Black women being around $5. But one thing is for sure, they can’t tell us our true worth.

I was so angry that tears started to well up in my eyes. How could I find my place in a system designed to oppress, depress, arrest, marginalize and criminalize, if not kill, people who look like me. There was a thin line between my love of law and my hatred for its unfair application. Bias and discrimination are so very hard to prove, but they are so very real. There is no system devoid of it, not the school system, the housing system, the healthcare system, the banking system or, of course, the legal system.

As I tried to look for the humane side of the law, I was offered a chance to visit some of the state jails with my criminal justice class. I refused. It wasn't a field trip for me, but rather a place connected to ill feelings. I had been to jails to visit loved ones a couple of times and disliked the process of even getting to see your people. I always left feeling sad. I didn't want to spend time in jails and courtrooms with the weight of fighting for folk's freedom, especially when that weight would be compounded by the weight of white privilege and the plight of the people on display.

Despite how strongly I felt, the opportunity to participate in a juvenile justice mentoring program called to me so I decided to volunteer at the MacLaren Youth Correctional Facility for a semester. These were young men that many had forgotten and labeled as unredeemable. The program involved mentoring young boys who had been harshly sentenced under Oregon's Measure 11 minimum sentencing policy, which directly and indirectly led to a 41% increase in the prison population in the first 10 years of its inception.

When I got to know them, I wondered what had happened to them. What had they seen and been through that made them think that their options were so limited? I still saw young boys and although I am sure that they may have been very angry and violent in some instances, when I got to know them and meet with them every week, I knew that there was good in their core. I truly believed that given the opportunity and the necessary support, a future success story was sitting right there in that room. Yes, those young men with a prison id number could later become a testimony for other troubled youth. They were still so very worth saving.

I was always preaching to those young men about the importance of going to school and how we need to "buy back the block." I also took the time to talk to them and really listen. The bottom line was though, they connected with me because I was almost always the only one in the group of students with even a glimmer of their background. Representation matters in mentoring too. I heard their stories, told some of mine, and we wrote a song together. They even got me to rap. It's funny that I have bars before I pass the bar, but it's on the way!

I got to know a young man who was 17-years-old and had been sentenced to 17 years in prison. His 15-year-old co-defendant told me, "You seem like you care. Law school probably mad hard, but we need people like you real bad." That young man re-inspired me! Despite how heavy the weights were I was carrying, I knew that I'd be an advocate for justice in some kind of way.

I had just wanted to go to law school and figure out a way to pay tuition, but I felt obligated to do more, especially when I learned that the school hadn't had an active Black Law Student Association (BLSA) chapter in a long time. Along with my colleagues, we organized a campus-wide protest with students of color, children, staff, the dean and allies. Interestingly, those pictures are still on the school's social media pages five pages later, which makes me wonder if there has been another protest or any activism since that time.

Michael Brown's death became a topic of discussion, sometimes lacking in sensitivity. The undergraduate campus had outbreaks of racist slurs written on campus common areas. My law school colleague, a white ally and I, decided to lend support to the young leaders. We both wanted to push for changes to policy but had different thoughts about how to go about achieving change. One of the freshmen leaders reminded me of my rebel with a cause self. She decided that she and 20 other students would occupy the president's house, refusing to leave. I was concerned about them getting arrested when I saw them coming in with sleeping bags, but fortunately the school supported the demonstration and allowed them to occupy the whole building for over a week.

Meanwhile on the law campus, we were holding candlelight vigils and hosting speak-up sessions that called for open dialogue about race and the law. The law school took the more subtle approach while the undergrads relied on more radical methods. Even during the turmoil though, there were points of light as shown by this beautiful photo of my son and an ally's son. I understood both methods because like Malcolm X said, "By any means necessary." But oh the things that were said in the open meeting.

There was only one Black, female professor at the law school. We had previously had several rather uncomfortable conversations. Her father was a police officer so she thought that my views on police were extreme and based on my own experiences and thus represented only a small handful according to her. In this particular meeting, she stood up to speak and I was hoping she would say something eloquently that I'd probably say harshly. Instead, she said something shocking I would not have said at all. She started off recounting how earlier in the week a student asked her how she was doing in light of all the racial tension on campus. She said, "Before they said this, I had forgot I was affected. It was like a reminder I am Black." She let out a light laugh before going on to say, "I am a woman first, not a Black woman, but a woman."

I was struggling with my facial expressions as many of my classmates eyes darted from her to me. My colleague, a young Black woman, stood up to speak after her. She was speaking a word, but about three sentences in she had a panic attack right there in front of them all. I felt her pain, but I went to the bathroom to have my panic attacks in solitude. I felt particularly concerned that they were allowed to witness what then felt like a temporary moment of weakness. As her friends ushered her out, I stood up to speak. I don't remember all I said, but I know I ended with, "I am a Black woman and I won't forget, nor do I want to."

Somewhere in there, an ally, an Asian woman who had become a strong advocate for both my son and me, stood up and started to share her views. (As a point of note, not only did she refer me to her sitter, she even let me drive her car before I managed to buy one.) She was visibly upset and gave an impassioned speech about being so sorry that she recruited us knowing there was not a support system or framework for Black students. If anything, we were sorry for her because we all knew what the deal was before deciding to attend a PWI. It isn't that we were happy with the lack of support, but we were unfortunately used to it. The bottom line was that these schools had a bottom line to meet and quotas to hit on the number of diverse students they give offers to and admit which is tied to the Federal funding they receive. If you can't pay, go see Sallie Mae they'd say. Between Uncle Sam and Aunt Sallie, I felt oppressed and very stressed. Not long after my colleague was ushered out, I stood up to say, "I think we should halt the meeting and resume dialog once students most impacted have had time to process in private." With that, the meeting was adjourned.

The next week we had a BLSA planning meeting. The president had very different views on how active we should be and how we should go about, or rather not go about, taking a stance and speaking out. He basically wanted to "remain neutral and fair." His neutrality was far too passive for me, but he was a Black man in leadership and I didn't want to rock the boat when all of our positions were so precarious.

When we left the meeting, the president of BLSA, who I thought of as "Dirty Dillan," was walking behind me with a small group of guys including only one other Black student. I knew he had some smart remarks to say so I walked even more powerfully, with my chin up. I didn't care what he said behind my back as long as he kept it respectful in my presence. I thought he knew better than to try me, but I apparently had given him too much credit or perhaps on that day he had a lapse in judgement. He called out, "Bye Felicia." I turned around with the quickness. I didn't do any neck or eye rolling, but said calmly, "You know my name. Choose Andrea or Ms. Thompson or better yet don't address me at all. You know I don't like you. I do my best to tolerate you, but you have no more times to make a bigger clown of yourself by making 'Black jokes' just for a few laughs from these white boys you keep begging for approval from. I won't call you an Oreo like I heard another student refer to you, but you are definitely one confused cookie." Everyone gasped and clutched their imaginary pearls. One said, "Oh my." I said, "Don't be alarmed now because it was just funny a minute ago when he called me Felicia."

I walked off, still feeling a little angry, but feeling slightly satisfied. Then I thought, "Why'd you have to go so hard? You could have ignored the man." My thoughts continued, "Naw, I had to say something. He went low and I went low and hit 'em with an uppercut." God was yet and is still working on me.

While we were in Portland, I'd take my son to the library down the street and afterward we'd go to the park. He seemed to always want to play with the white kids and their dads, to the point that I'd get up from looking over legal briefs to play with him so he would not intrude on them. Usually they smiled and said it was no problem, but Portland had a subtle type of indirect discrimination that taught me not to simply take things at face value because it's in the looks, thoughts and inaction, not the talk.

At first I thought it was just a part of him longing for more of his Dad's presence, but when I increased the flights back home I realized that he didn't initiate play with Black men in similar settings. So I asked, "Jeremiah, why do you always play with the men at the park in Portland, but you don't even acknowledge the men at the park here?" Without a pause, my then seven-year-old son said, "Ma, white men are nice and Black men are mean. White men always smiling and playing with their dogs and Black men be frowning and looking mean." After the initial shock, I felt sorrow ... I thought to myself he doesn't know that they smile at him now but some can see him as a threat when he's a pre-teen and those dogs, yeah it wasn't nice when they used them on our people.

It was a challenge to try to explain the (wicked) way of the world to my young son. I had to take baby steps. I said, "Jeremiah, there are some nice people and there are some mean people. White does not mean nice and black doesn't mean ... mean. No matter what you see, know that there are good people, but also know that some people will never be good people." I knew I needed to say more, but I couldn't find the words. I knew based on his experiences he was justified in believing that all Black men were mean, even if I knew it wasn't true. He will one day be a Black man, and Lord knows I always told him to be kind especially with how he treated young ladies.

I made it my business from that point on to use all of my business resources to get my son around positive influences. It wasn't long before I started to make connections and contacts in the city. I'd met and developed a great relationship with the only Black woman to serve as a Judge in the Federal Court. Like my Grandmother, she was also from

Arkansas. The first time Grandma came to Oregon, they clicked over peach cobbler and ice cream. I couldn't believe a Black woman Judge was sitting in my living room, live in the flesh, laughing over peach cobbler! This woman had dark skin like me and a shaped up afro too. She didn't speak bashfully in front of "them," nor did she laugh at all their jokes, only the ones she seemed to genuinely find funny. She had attained all this success in white Portlandia and still managed not to conform to what they wanted her to be. Instead of trying to fit the mold, she broke and reshaped it so that it would be inclusive of students like me. I knew then more than ever that anything was possible. She was a trailblazer and I was ready to follow in her footsteps while blazing my own trail. Seeing that role model pushed me even harder.

I had almost eight weeks between having to move out of our old place and the time the new place would become available. Fortunately, my legal writing professor had grown fond on me and was aware of my situation. She and her family were traveling for the school break so she allowed me to stay at her house for nearly two weeks. It was a nice minimalist home, but definitely fancy in its own way, crisp and chic. I felt odd being in someone else's home, but I knew that it was temporary and that God had a place for me. When she came back, my favorite Judge from Arkansas talked to the State's Attorney and convinced her to let me stay in her basement for the remaining weeks. It was not as far from campus as the Judge's home so it was easier for me to get to school and back. It was in a quiet residential area that made for the best morning walks.

I was feeling kind of low about having to move into the basement of someone else's home as a grown woman and a mother, but on one morning walk God showed me that there was purpose in the struggle and I still had so very much to be grateful for. I'd noticed a woman that got coffee around the same time that I took my morning meditation walks. She didn't stand out much; I just recognized her as a regular. I kept seeing a station wagon on the next block that had lots of boxes in it. One morning I got out earlier than normal and to my surprise the woman was sleeping in her car. Like someone had turned on a faucet, the tears flowed—tears of shame for having been so ungrateful to complain about my having to live in the basement of a half a million dollar home while just on the next block, a woman was sleeping in her car.

I didn't want her to know I saw her, but I wondered about her. How did she end up in the car? Was she a mother? I didn't have much, but I wondered how I could help. God put it on my heart to leave an envelope with a note of encouragement and $10. It was only enough for three morning coffees or a quarter tank of gas, but I'm sure it warmed her heart and fueled her just the same, or at least I hoped it did. From that point on, whenever I felt down about my situation I reminded myself that it could be worse and also that it was getting better. It was also at that time I discovered an online broadcasting tool called Periscope that would literally change the trajectory of my life. It's no longer active, but the connections and experience I gained on it live on.

Having my son with me was a source of great comfort. I would see him looking at me while I studied, as he took a break from his homework. Even amidst dry, dustless tomes, I would smile thinking my son had already been to law school before he even graduated from elementary school. A few times my son fell asleep on the computer in the Judge's chambers while I was in the middle of heated mock trials to earn extra scholarship money and see if I wanted courtroom practice or transactional practice. I learned how to hold my own amongst people designated to be attorneys before they were christened. When they were asked what they wanted to be when they grew up, the answers were not pie in the sky but real possibilities to consider and work towards, from preppy pre-kindergartens to college preparatory schools to trust-funded journeys on the Harvard and Yale pathways that their people had trodden for several

generations. I was determined to give my son the same opportunities by forging the way.

With that resolution, there were so many obstacles, some subtle and some very overt. The very first time I had an issue at my son's school was in preschool when he forgot his lunch. Instead of the teacher calling me or providing him with something to eat, I first learned he had gone all day without eating when I went to pick him up. He had even sat at the table while the other children were eating during lunch time. I was enraged, but I knew that teacher already appeared to be extremely nervous and uncomfortable when speaking with me so as gently as I could, I asked, "Why didn't you make any attempt to get a hungry child food some kind of way? The law campus is all of two blocks away." I told her that I'd worked in a daycare and couldn't imagine not going in my pocket if necessary or at least contacting the parent to ensure a child did not go hungry.

I followed up with an email to the directors, but Dramatic Daisy had already played the victim role with tears and full theatrics claiming that I seemed angry and intimidating. I said it as nicely as I could and was still labeled the "angry Black woman." Particularly when you stand up on policy, white women often play the victim.

I started touring firms and shadowing attorneys and quickly realized that the reason the law firms had all of the amenities including chefs, showers, and sleeping quarters was because they intended for you to live at work. That was not what I wanted at all! I didn't really get the total picture clearly though until I had posted in a lawyer's group that I was looking for a used vehicle to purchase. One of them responded and said, "I've been out of law school for two years and I still haven't bought a car because I decided to pay off my student loans first rather than spend money on insurance and gas. Have you thought about reallocating that money to paying down the interest on your loans while you're in school?" While I understood her response, I couldn't help but think to myself, "Honey, you don't know my situation." I responded and told her that I had a young son and couldn't bear another winter on the bus. Of course, I couldn't help but think that maybe I was on the wrong path. If she was in the profession I was working towards, and couldn't afford a car two years after graduating, something was wrong. I was spending a lot of time and money on a degree to make about the same as I did as a manager before law school. Make it make sense!

That same week, I attended a law firm anniversary celebration after being invited by Julie, one of the best female defense attorneys in the state. She was a white woman and definitely an advocate and ally for equal and human rights. I normally felt comfortable in white spaces when she was in the room. This time things went drastically different. One of the attorneys, a white man, had a little too much to drink and got much too friendly with a couple of younger students that happened to be white females. I observed from afar noting how uncomfortable the young ladies looked as he made suggestive remarks and subtle but intrusive touches. They nervously grinned at his lackluster jokes, while I cringed hoping that his eyes wouldn't turn to me next. Unfortunately, they did. In front of a room full of white people, he said out loud, "I like your hair. It's sexy ... Can I touch it?" Before I could answer, he was already stroking my long twists in a way that made me freeze up. I took a nervous step back not knowing exactly what to say or do. For the first time in a long time, I was completely speechless.

Julie quickly halted her conversation and made it over to me sensing that something had gone wrong. She said, "Andrea, are you okay?" I didn't respond. Hearing her say my name again seemed to snap me out of my daze. As strong as I was, I had tears in my eyes—not so much because I was mad at him (I was), but more so because I was mad I didn't respond with that fire I knew I had. And I was mad that I didn't stand up for myself. He'd managed to make me feel small, powerless, and voiceless. Julie said, "Come on, let me get you a ride home."

I went home and told Grandma what happened. She was mad as hell too. She said, "You should've said something. I didn't raise you not to speak up! You don' took a wooden nickel." When she said that, I felt like Caine in *Menace II Society*. The crooked counselor was actually the menace to society, but I was the one in the interrogation room with OG

Granny saying, "You know you done f'd up, don't you?"

I was sick of Portland. I mean, my school had bias discussions and Black student support, but it was so overwhelmingly white, making it inherently non-Black, that sometimes it was just hard to BE. Like Tupac said, I kept my head up, but I was often FED UP. The tough girl, now the tough Mom, often felt like it was me and my baby boy against the world. I knew that I fit nearly every stereotype. I was a Black woman walking around campus with my baby, with no father in sight. I was from the hood, and although it wasn't like Cabrini-Green, they looked at it just the same. It didn't matter that I grew up on the southside of Chicago in proximity to the University of Chicago. If people got shot and killed on a fairly regular basis where you lived, it was the ghetto. Period. While there was often a difference in mindset if not zip code, it didn't matter to most people. Hell, it just started mattering to the university enough to get a trauma center there, but I digress.

I actually understated it above. I was **past** sick of Portland and its illness wouldn't let me be silent about it. I had the sometimes ponderous responsibility of speaking out because in that space I represented more than just me. I was frozen to near silence when it happened, but I was compelled to speak out boldly in the aftermath. I got on the computer and clacked those keys rapidly, expressing every bit of what I felt in the moment but was too taken aback to say. I tried my best not to be confrontational, not wanting to be dubbed the "angry Black woman," but I was already labeled that and I affirmed it for them every time I spoke passionately. And, yes, people often confuse passion for anger where we are concerned.

By the time I completed my email, I felt relieved, exhausted, but still relieved. The weight was slightly lifted. My emotions had poured out of me onto the keyboard. I came out of my bedroom that had become my office because I did more work than I got sleep and instead of the wine I wanted, Grandma gave me the slice of pie I needed. She went in on me and fueled me up only to come back with a slice of sweet potato pie to make the sour time turn sweet. More to the point, her not so gentle push had helped me get my voice and power back. And I would not be taking any more wooden nickels.

## Connection Clue

Have you harbored resentment for a situation that you thought you should have responded to differently? Maybe in the moment you couldn't bring yourself to respond like you thought you would?

Have you had to delay what you thought was an imperative part of God's plan for your life? How could that delay actually serve as preparation? Reflect on the ways in which it could actually be a way to better position yourself even more powerfully!

**Audacity Affirmation**

I resist the urge to do things in my own timing and surrender to God's timing, knowing that His plan and foresight are much greater than my own. He is the supreme orchestrator of time and works all things together for my good. Even delays are refining me, not defying or defining me. I forgive myself for not taking action in times when the crisis caused me to freeze. I am strong when I am still. I am strong when I activate. I will further develop my gifts and activate my growth process by feeding my mind, body and spirit with things that will nurture my ability to overcome!

# Chapter 6

# Faith Under Fire

Now faith is the substance of things hoped for,
the evidence of things not seen.
Hebrews 11:1

**"I've had the opportunity to lose everything twice. In each situation, all I could do was turn to God. God allowed me to come back, and the comeback was more significant and more substantial than any loss could have ever been. God has sustained me. God has allowed me to grow amid challenges. God spoke to my spirit, which allowed me to change my mind and pivot. So I am clear, God is the Ultimate Plug!"**

**—Marki Lemons-Ryhal**

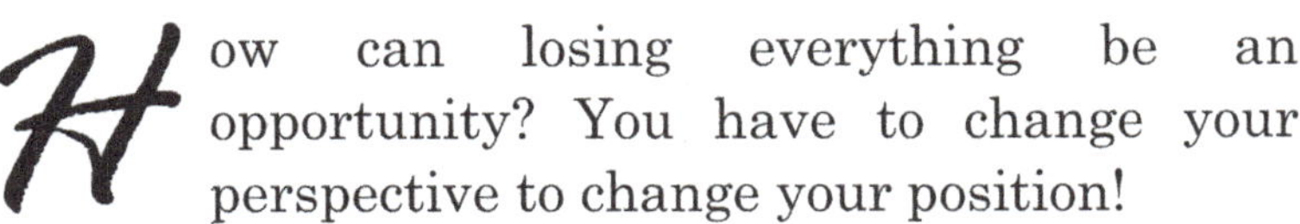

How can losing everything be an opportunity? You have to change your perspective to change your position!

## The Valley Experience: 90 Days Homeless

During the most challenging times, I felt like I was on standby waiting for my name to be called while on a layover far from my destination. Then, even when I got the clearance to onboard, we began taxiing while waiting for takeoff. You're ready to experience the air and soar above the clouds, but based on conditions you're temporarily restricted to the runway as opposed to standing up and staying down for the journey. I could say more on that, but I choose to go high when people and politicians go low. Admittedly, over the years, I've struggled with Michelle O's quote, "When they go low, we go high." They've been going so low for so long that it's like submarine level. Is it ever permissible to just gon' and get low 'cause for sure you can't let them come for you and just get away with it? Well, vengeance is the Lord's and in the paraphrasing of Jay-Z, "Don't argue with a fool because from a distance folks can't tell who is who." So, soar high when they go submarine low.

> **"I have the audacity to believe that peoples everywhere can have three meals a day for their bodies, education and culture for their minds, and dignity, equality, and freedom for their spirits."**
>
> **—Dr. Martin Luther King, Jr.**

Quality housing, or rather the lack thereof, affects every area of one's life. It threatens to compromise safety, security, health and education. I learned that (theoretically) studying in South Africa and (practically) one cold winter in Chicago. It broke my heart seeing Will Smith portray a Dad struggling to keep his dream and hope alive while also raising his son in *The Pursuit of Happyness*. Rock bottom for them came when they slept in the bathroom of a train station. Mine came on a CTA bus. My son had gone to work with me and by the time we got on the bus we were both tired. I knew to sit by the driver where I could be seen in his mirror but not too close to the doors. It was so cold I had my purse tucked under two layers of coats. My son fell asleep on my arm. All I remember was saying a prayer as I held his hand, and the next thing I knew the driver was waking me up saying it was his last run. I woke up alarmed by his voice, but I was comforted that it was him and not one of the men that rode the buses at night. He said, "I knew you were tired, so I didn't wake you." We had been riding on his route for two hours! He continued, "The next bus doesn't come for over 30 minutes. You can wait on here until I have to head to the garage so you don't have to wake little man up right now." A few minutes later, he apologetically said, "I have to pull off, but the bus shelter across the street is where you will need to wait and you have about 17 more minutes."

I said thank you and went to carry my son off the bus. He was heavy, but I'd rather carry him to the bus stop bench and sit and hold him than for him to wake up and feel like we were deserted in the cold night. It was enough that I felt that way! My efforts were in vain. He woke up. Really, I was relieved because I couldn't make it across the street carrying him. I had hand warmers in his gloves and took off one of my coats to cover him. Those 17 minutes went by like a snail, but I prayed each and every minute that somehow God would carry us over this valley and keep us on the way.

I was too talented to be this low, but God told me right there in the cold of the night on the bus stop that these trying times were only temporary and He would manage to use even it to prepare me for my next. I couldn't understand it and I surely felt like I was a big dreamer just like Nana said. Even under the circumstances though, I was faithful that my valley would lead to the victory. I still had something of unique value. God could still use me even as I stood in need of a miracle. Fortunately, God is still in the miracle business. I would need to hold on to that belief many times during my journey.

Before I became a mother, shortly after I returned home from undergrad school, I lived in a mixed-income community formerly known as the Ida B. Wells Housing Project. The irony is that I lived in the projects just north of there in my early childhood years, went to Holy Angels school a block away, and had fond memories of riding through The Wells (as we called them) on the ice cream truck my Granddaddy owned. It was the only stop where he didn't let me get off the truck at all. I'm ashamed to say that I didn't really learn about the enormity of the legacy of Ida B. Wells until much later in life when I studied the work of great Black women abolitionists and writers. It is interesting how we can occupy spaces named after such powerful people and not realize the significance of the person's contribution.

Paw Paw would drive down King Drive, the history route he called it. He'd point out houses that prominent singers sang at and talked about Black-owned businesses like Gerri's Palm Tavern and Bacon's Hat Shop. When he was telling all those "old stories," I didn't understand much about the importance or the depth of the knowledge he was really dropping, but I loved the way that Paw Paw told stories about music, history and education. He brought you into the story and with excitement you could see his passion and love for people, particularly our people and our history.

My Grandad gave out ice cream and "polishes" to the kids over there once a week. They were the real have nots; others were just scammers trying to get over. I was about eight when I remember my Grandad caught me sneaking a boy at Mount Carmel a free polish sausage because he told me some sob story about being hungry and not having any money. He told the young man, "You should be ashamed of yourself conning my lil' granddaughter's caring heart." He threatened to tell the school if the boy didn't clean the steamer racks for him. The kid did it too. He didn't want no steam or no smoke.

Paw Paw looked at me with a stern face and said, "You have seen the real have nots. That kid is just trying to get a free ride. If a man don't work, he don't eat. Don't you make it easy on them and you damn sure don't pay their way." I was able to understand that for real when I got older long after he passed, but even then I felt it down in my young shondo as I uttered, "Okay, I'm sorry Paw Paw."

When Paw Paw got older and stopped working on the trucks, he'd sing for us at family events. His favorites were "Hold On To What You've Got!" by Joe Tex and "This Is A Man's World" by James Brown. Long after Paw Paw had passed, I heard the version of the song with James Brown and Pavarotti. I cried because I finally understood that the song wasn't diminishing a woman's value by saying that this is a man's world and times sure have changed, yet some things remain the same.

One of those things is, as Paw Paw taught me, if you don't work you can't eat, but later I came to realize if you don't have a place to cook the meal, it can be difficult to eat. I started writing what I thought would be my first book (now my next book) by candlelight when I had to choose between rent and lights which left me without lights for 10 days. There was no hallway plug to run the cord to like I'd seen growing up, but I managed because I stored food in the fridge of a vacant apartment. We had a private room at the library, and we ate real good from the cafeteria. I would study all night while my son slept on a cot. I saved money on groceries because my senior friend that worked there started turning her head the other way when she saw me with my Tupperware. She said, "Baby, your tuition pays for the food, and I see you studying with that baby." She even told me when to come on her shifts.

I kept going like it really wasn't a big deal, but it was. I felt like a loser. I'd come across the country only to struggle. My child wasn't even school age yet, and I could barely afford tuition. Some days, I remember being so down on myself and being so incredibly sad. Other days, I remember singing, "Encourage Yourself," which made me feel like there was for certain a blessing attached to my broken places.

I had given up on law school. I mean my heart was still in it, but I'd grown so tired of Portland being so white in and outside of the classroom. I'd grown weary of being the one to speak up and out when we'd discover how the law was so incredibly biased. I got tired and so I made the decision to move back home and further my business and other ventures.

Before it got bad, I tried to do something major. I had gotten a settlement check from a life-saving situation. I had the money, but not the credit. Three people I knew needed to move. I went to one of the elders in the family and shared my plan. I wanted to get my real estate license reinstated as it had expired. I felt like it really was time to "possess the land" and even with bad credit I was determined to put some kind of plan in place.

Shortly after that, I learned that the mini-mansion that my family on my Dad's side somehow lost was up for sale. I knew better than to ask how much it sold for, but what I was able to find out was that it sold for only back taxes when I was a baby and then $100k when I was a kid. Now I was a grad student and it was on the market for over $700k. The story was the same gentrification story that plagues a lot of our folks. What I saw clearly was I was mad behind the scheduled plan that I had when I was 12 of getting rich and buying back Grandma Jenkins' house. I had a whole plan that we could rent out the third level to college students, and do Airbnb out of the coach house while using the first level and the basement as a business incubator. In the kitchen, we would record content for Live In The Content Kitchen™.

I couldn't acquire nor afford a $700,000 mortgage, but I had the audacity to reach out to the owners anyway. Somehow I managed to get the owner's email address. I started by reminding him about a little girl on a pink and white bike who once asked him about not removing the names carved in the slab of pavement in front of the home. My family had carved their names in the concrete. In fact, my Cousin even put his footprint in it. Surprisingly, he remembered and invited me to the house to meet him and his wife when I came home. The house was immaculate. Despite my financial deficit, I had the nerve to ask them to consider a land contract that was like a lower risk rent to own, or so I was advised based on the questions I asked industry experts after a couple of months of research.

Long deal short, I wanted to help my people buy a building. I was going to be the agent on the deal, and use the commission towards repairs. The result would be three units to use for vacation rentals and one to live in. The deal was almost done; the meeting was set. Afterwards, someone suggested that it was too big of an investment for an ol' lady to make with me. Eventually, the elder told me to get the building myself and then they would invest with me. I thought about that and wondered whether we have to struggle solo then come up for people to then say, "OK, now I'll build with you." Surely there must be people who can see the big picture, and help grow it from seed to fruit so the harvest will be for the good of everyone. I mean where are the visionaries and builders? Apparently, I had to go low to come up rather than maintaining and partnering to sustain and grow. I realized I would have to create the manual, the blueprint, and be the builder all at the same time—or so it seemed.

Ironically, we later found out that the elder had moved into a senior building that was family-owned (by someone else's family). Everyone was related, from the property manager to the leasing manager down to the janitor. I said, "You didn't want to invest in your family's portfolio so you're paying rent to help them build their family's legacy." Frustrated with me, she responded, "Oh hush gal, you need to know something about all that kind of stuff, and you just talkin' and dreamin' with no money to back it up." I had earned a degree, had gotten a real estate sales license, and worked in property management for nearly five years, but still in her eyes I wasn't qualified enough.

Let me tell you something, sometimes it is those who they least expect to do a great work that the Lord will position and use in a mighty way that will leave others in awe and serve as a representation of what nobody but God can do. Your overcoming is a testament to His goodness! And let me tell you something else. I never wanted it to be this hard for the ones after me. Maybe I'd go from not having a place to being the owner of several places. But until then I had to start from the bottom to get there.

My savings quickly dwindled. It wasn't a whole lot, but it was getting low and spent on basics. I couldn't stay in the space I was in. I had to make a choice and I didn't have a lot of options. I had to make a bold move and go lower first in order to go higher. There was a purpose even in that! Building a skyscraper requires a solid foundation and that requires digging, hence you must go low first. But on that foundation, a mighty thing that will serve many can be built. Even in a homeless shelter, I was rich while broke. Yes, I stayed in a homeless shelter, y'all! Yes me! How did I make it through? Because it seems that no matter how low I fell and how numb I became, I still had a mustard seed of faith that God could and would turn it all around for my good.

And Jesus said unto them, Because of your unbelief: for verily I say unto you, If ye have faith as a grain of mustard seed, ye shall say unto this mountain, Remove hence to yonder place; and it shall remove; and nothing shall be impossible unto you.
Matthew 17:20

People often make the presumption that domestic violence and struggle have to look a certain way. They were confused when there was no drug abuse (keeping it real, a little marijuana use, but no abuse). They assumed you were uneducated, or that you must have done something wrong or been something that you were ashamed of.

One would think in my hometown I had to have other places to go. The first night there was a week after my son's birthday. I wrestled with the idea of going to stay with "friends." I had already tried staying with one family member and that wasn't gonna happen again. I thought back to when I went away to school and my Mom told me before we left to hit the road "to do well 'cause I didn't have anywhere to come back to." I wondered if I had made the right decision in coming back home. I had survived in each of the other states I lived in, but it was in a place I called home that the best place to be was actually a shelter.

Despite this, I knew I had to do something drastically different to cause a shift to catapult me into a newness that would allow me to walk in my destiny with less weight. I honestly didn't feel broke.

I didn't have a lot, but somehow I felt that I was on the brink of something major and even this would be used in my testimony. I felt that, I saw that and I believed that. The trouble was holding on to that belief when those closest to me took it as an opportunity to instill doubt. I heard the murmurs both directly and indirectly. I was called a homeless B%&*#. Folks made snide remarks like "all that education and now she ain't got nothing to show for it." I had an associate try to embarrass me about my situation and I was confused because she lived in the second unit of her mama's building with her child's father. My Mama didn't have a building, but surely she wasn't in a position to look down on me from where she was living.

I started praying every time they talked bad about me, even if it meant praying out loud. My biggest motivation came from the doubt and spiteful words of some of the people closest to me. I let the doubt, negative words, and ignorance motivate me to dream bigger than my surroundings would suggest was possible. I had the nerve to dream rich dreams with only a couple dollars in my pocket!

When I wasn't able to do for people like I could when I had a corporate job, those same people started talking down to me in every way, and they were vulgar with it too. From raising my son on my own to being broke in business to, "If you so smart, why you struggling?" I heard it all. I saw students with far less talent and not even one brilliant idea come home from school and get more support from their people. In my low moments, I started to believe that maybe my ambitions were too lofty and maybe God had forgotten about me. I mean, I was about to walk into a shelter with my son holding my hand. I felt like I had failed, but the more I heard the things they taunted and teased me about, the more I was determined to overcome. I asked God to give me the courage and strength not to cry, to go through, and to be strong.

I had asked a lady for part-time work that would allow me to work on major accounts and still build my business. She dropped us off at the shelter after work. It was dark and the night was still. Walking up the ramp, it almost felt like I was in a dream. I looked back at her concerned face and reassured her that we were okay. We were, physically, but emotionally I was confused. I wondered how I was still walking, why I didn't break. When I walked in the door, I thought I would break but I didn't. I wondered when I would. Just then my son squeezed my hand as if he knew exactly what I was feeling. He looked up at me and out of nowhere said, "We have so many adventures Mama. I'm just happy to be with you wherever we go." I knew in that moment that God was sending word through my baby.

The first night I managed to hold in the tears. The second night, I held them in until my son went to sleep. I didn't sleep much. I stayed up at night working on my laptop, researching how to grow my business. I was literally running a struggling business from a shelter, and with a free government phone at that. My resiliency was foolish to some, yet amazing to me. I cried a couple times, but surprisingly I wasn't depressed. Most of the time, I was extremely hopeful! I felt rich while I was broke—like I was fractured, but still functioning. There had been times when I had plenty of money and felt worse, so I took it in stride and held my head up high.

I sent a request for a pass to go to Atlanta for a conference. **The Director asked if I was going to meet a man. I laughed and said, "I'm going to meet some money and make some business connections."** I showed her the conference agenda and my plane ticket. I said, "Ma'am, I'm really in pursuit of something big regardless of my current circumstances. I can't afford to have my wings clipped right now." She approved the pass.

My son and I had a room to ourselves at first. After the first week, a young lady got into an altercation with her roommate and she and her son ended up becoming our roommates. She was young (around 22 or 23), loud and ready to fight if necessary. She actually reminded me of myself when

I was her age, and had striking similarities to my younger sister. For some reason, she was so respectful to me. She complained about the food and the staff. I just listened. She even started asking me about her goals of doing hair and makeup and maybe owning a shop one day. I wondered why she talked to me so differently than she did with the rest of the ladies.

Once we had gotten to know each other better, she said, "You cool. When you first came here, we thought that you were undercover." I asked what she meant and she went on to explain that she and a few of the other women had determined that I wasn't really homeless, but was there to secretly observe the staff. I got a real good laugh out of that and thought to myself, "Hell, I'm homeless too!" I laughed and said, "Why, 'cause I got this laptop? Well, I'm homeless with a laptop!" The fact that I could crack a joke about it let me know that I really did have crazy faith. Even when you are in a dark place, your light will still shine.

We talked about it a bit more because I was still a little shocked, but it finally made sense why they kept telling me about the processes and staff. I laughed again and said, "Girl, I'm here 'cause I need help too. I'm in the same situation as y'all." She said, "Girl, no you not. You are about to go to Atlanta, not to strip or nothing crazy but for a business conference. You might be here with us but you're not in the same situation. You gonna be alright. I wouldn't bet on nobody here, but I'd bet on you."

There I was trying to inspire her, and she was being an inspiration to me.

I went upstairs and asked my roommate if I could pay her to braid my hair. She said, "Yeah, girl, and I'll even do it on a discount." I thanked her and left to go to the beauty supply store before picking my son up from school. I didn't have a car and we were pretty far from his school. The only good thing about being in that situation is I was able to enroll my son in a Level 1 school near his doctor's office due to a Federal Law that was locally referred to as the STLS program (Students in Temporary Living Situations). Advocating for your child as a single mother in the public school setting is a challenge in itself (more on that in the "Overcoming Injustice" and "Audacity of Saving Grace" chapters).

When I made it back from the beauty supply store, my roommate seemed a bit sad. We chatted about her life, her girlfriend, and why she didn't trust men. I shared with her how I found it to be so crazy how many men I knew had never had their own place to stay. They go from their mama's basement and then from girlfriend to girlfriend, never getting anything more than a cell phone bill in their name, let alone a lease. At least I could be thankful that my son's father didn't take our son to the women's homes. He opted instead for infrequent Mickey D's and quick Target toy runs. It seemed as if that "at least" mentality was something to be thankful for. Far too often, I'd heard, "at least" be glad that he comes around sometimes because other kids hadn't seen their fathers in years. According to them, it was absurd of me to ask for more than the bare minimum. Mediocracy somehow became the new standard, but that's a whole 'nother story.

On the flight to Atlanta and all the way back, I gave what my roommate said to me a lot of thought. I kept circling back to this, "If I was so smart and wasn't supposed to be there, just why was I there?" What was the point of God positioning me in a shelter of all places? Why did I have to go through this after all I had invested in my success story? I didn't know the answers, but I was committed to staying strong and keeping the faith. I wasn't about to believe that I didn't have something in me that God could use. Yes, even in the shelter, I had something in my hand. I didn't understand why, but I was gonna get through it so I could see the purpose in it.

When I returned to Chicago, I met with Jan, the resident social worker and she told me, "I don't want you to think you're the exception. You're here because you need help, just like everybody else." I responded, "You're right; I am not the exception, but I AM exceptional. I am ordinary yet extraordinary." I said it without thinking. She smirked and said, "Okayyyy, Miss Thompson!" as if she halfway believed in my resolve and halfway wanted to laugh at me.

As Oprah says, one thing I know for sure is that some people will not believe I had the audacity to start building my business while I was in a homeless shelter, but I have never been short of audacity! A prospective client considering a contract for publicity and social media management services contacted me asking to speak with me as soon as possible. It struck me as odd because he had never reached out to me via video chat. I was having a challenging morning so I was listening to inspirational speeches to muster the hope of even a mustard seed. I called him back and he started off slowly but firmly which alerted me as it was different from his comical norm. He said, "Ms. Andrea, I was in a meeting with a colleague and mentioned working with you and was told that you're an assault survivor and are currently, or were recently, living at a domestic violence shelter." I was confused as my mind went from anger to shame wondering who had exposed my secret. I just wanted to struggle in silence and come back with a win and somebody had sabotaged my plan, probably for their own selfish agenda. I couldn't hold in the tears anymore. I wasn't just shedding tears. I was sobbing uncontrollably. I couldn't let him see me like that so I disconnected the call. He texted back and asked to pray for and with me. I called back when I got myself together. The cat was now out of the bag and after my next jump like a lucky cat, I was hoping I'd land on my feet.

Everyone in the shelter had to pick a day of the week to prepare lunch or dinner. Often, I would be excused because of my work schedule. Breakfast was my favorite meal of the day and I missed having Sunday sit down breakfasts with my son. I quickly grew tired of the cold cereal, bruised fruit and nearly expired yogurt they were serving. I decided that cooking breakfast on the weekends would establish some sense of normalcy for me and my son. I didn't initially realize how it would help the others out too. One morning I woke up super early and went downstairs to start cooking. The house mom rushed in to stop me saying I could only cook on my scheduled days and if I did I had to have enough for everyone. I said, "I have enough to stretch a meal this time and I will be sure to get enough for everyone going forward." Begrudgingly she said, "Okay, but since you haven't been officially approved to do this, let's just keep it between us." She later came back and chatted with me while I was cooking, and then she casually and almost bashfully said, "That food sure is smellin' good. Gimmie a plate too." She was not the nicest person, but somehow a homecooked, country-style breakfast seemed to enhance her disposition.

I started cooking breakfast every Sunday. It was therapeutic for me to come down to the kitchen early, play my gospel music and cook a big breakfast before waking up my son to the familiar smell of grits, eggs, cinnamon rolls and fresh fruit. It wasn't long before the other mothers started using their food stamps to contribute to breakfast. The house mom said they had never done that. The food seemed to bring us together.

It wasn't until a few weeks later that I fully realized how God was using me through preparing breakfast. A woman who had been known for walking with her head down and staying in her room came out and joined us. She was sitting down talking and for the first time I saw her smile. She even laughed. My roommate started coming down early in the morning to make breakfast with me. I thought she was coming to help cook, but I soon realized she just wanted to talk. I'd be cooking and listening with gospel playing lightly in the background. "Is that Fantasia?" she asked one day. I said, "Yep." I couldn't really sing, but my spirit belted out, "The Lord is blessing me right now." She said, "Even in a shelter!?" I said, "Yeah, the Lord is still blessing us even right now." She said, "I didn't think you'd be able to make those pear-glazed cinnamon rolls when I looked at that bag of old pears. You sure know how to take a lil' bit and stretch it." I said, "See, I told you God was still blessing us." (See the "Audacious Recipes" section for a taste of the sweetness that God can bring to ***every*** situation.)

We both smiled and out of nowhere the tough girl exterior cracked and gave me a hug. I knew how much she must have trusted me to let me in. I knew because I was a tough girl too. Sometimes all a tough girl needs though is a hug and a kind word from somebody who genuinely cares. It was in that moment that I realized these meals were more than just food. It was a blessing that created community and fed the people's spirit. I knew then that God was still using me, even in that shelter.

Halloween was the first and technically the only "holiday" we spent in the shelter. It felt like we were in a nightmare, but we weren't on Elm Street. Despite the despair that I sometimes felt amidst bursts of determination, I resolved to still make an effort to create good memories for my son. I hit two birds with one stone by buying my son a puffy vest from a local thrift store that would double as both a fall jacket and a Halloween costume. I cut out a number three, took one of his baseball caps and sewed it on the front, drew him a mustache with my eyeliner and voilà my baby was "Chance the Rapper" for Halloween!

At my next meeting with Jan the social worker, she told me there were vacancies at Parkway Gardens. She told me to go complete the application and I might be able to get on their priority waitlist. I didn't want to sound ungrateful, as they already thought that I needed to come to grips with the fact that I was homeless and didn't have many choices, so I simply agreed. It wasn't like I was from the suburbs, but Parkway was even more hood than my hood. Although I grew up less than three miles away from there, Parkway was known for gang activity and violence, on top of being surrounded by poorly performing schools. I knew a few people who were either killed in Parkway or killed by someone from there.

When I got there, I walked through the complex and felt like crying. I saw so many bonnet babies and pajama pimps ... no judgement (I stand with Monique though), and I just felt heavy and that it wasn't for me. Something definitely wasn't right, yet I said to myself, "How a homeless person gon' be picky?" I went into the office and asked for the manager Jan told me to see. She handed me the application on a clipboard. Something about the sound of that metal clasp hitting the clipboard made me feel like I was having an out-of-body experience. I sat down and as I wrote my name in on the top line, I heard, "You don't belong here. I have something better for you. Do you trust me or the social worker?"

I immediately got up and handed her the clipboard and said, "Thanks, but I'm going to come back another day." The woman looked confused and replied, "I can't guarantee that there will be a unit for you when you do." I said, "I understand." After I walked out, tears started rolling down my face and I said, "There's a unit for me somewhere, but it ain't here." I had been telling my son that we were in camp. I figured I needed to tell myself that too. My self-talk became, "This is not permanent. You are not homeless. You are homeFULL and in transition."

God gave me a glimpse that confirmed what my spirit felt, but my eyes had yet to see. Christmas was quickly approaching. I still hadn't found a place, but

I was faithful that God would somehow provide. I had referrals to three different organizations that offered housing assistance, but it seemed as if I was able to find more options on my own than the agencies did. I heard God saying, "I will provide from an unlikely source." I trusted Him even though what I was going through didn't make sense to anyone. I didn't know quite how it would work together for my good, but I believed it would, somehow, some way. God has a way of sending you a peak promise in a valley moment. Trouble will transform you and the valley can lead to the victory! I can hear Yolanda Adams singing "The Battle Is Not Yours" in my spirit because I know God is a giant slayer!

One of the agencies I was hoping would help me secure permanent housing called and offered me the chance to stay in a presidential suite at one of the fanciest hotels on the Magnificent Mile. I had actually hosted my first business conference on the Magnificent Mile. I was beyond grateful for the opportunity as I had felt sad the previous week because it would be the first time my son wouldn't have a Christmas tree. I had prayed that somehow God would still make it a really special Christmas for him.

The social worker called and asked me to write a thank you letter that included my story, some requests for my son including toys he liked and his clothing size. I took it as an opportunity to submit a well-written letter telling my story my way that would also show I had researched the hotel's philanthropic endeavors. I asked for things that would really help change our circumstances. I knew it was a long shot, but I asked for two shares of stock in the hotel for my son, a RideShare gift card, a laptop, and paid tutoring services for my son. I told them that my son liked books and Legos. I also wrote that I had applied for a job with one of the partner hotels to see if I could persuade them to give me an interview.

The penthouse was beautiful and elaborately decorated with a Christmas tree! God made a way for us to have one in spite of our current circumstances. I was so excited just to see my son's excitement. We started opening gifts.

I was so incredibly grateful, but I immediately wondered how we would get all those items to our already packed storage in zero below weather when we checked out. I looked at the house shoes and with tears in my eyes I promised we would not be in that situation much longer. I thought, "I'll save the house shoes for when I get my place." As nice of a gesture as it all was, I knew that the people who orchestrated it didn't really know the depths of someone's needs when they are in a housing crisis. How do you give house shoes to someone without a house?! Don't get me wrong though; I was excited for our blessing. I called and invited my Grandma to come down and see how God had made a way even amidst my struggle. When she arrived, she excitedly said, "We downstairs," and I realized that she'd brought others with her. What they saw as a celebratory moment, and undoubtedly an opportunity to peek into my pain, was really only a temporary relief from a very real crisis.

Checkout time came and here we were sitting in the lobby with a cartful of boxes and bags. My son was still excited and that kept me from feeling the weight of our temporary fairytale ending. He looked at me and said, "Mommy, we got to play rich for a little while!" I said, "Well baby, I am working hard so we don't have to 'play' rich, but can live wealthy. Some businesses start off rough, but we're going to get a nice place and then we'll get a car again too! We gon' be alright!" He said, "I know Mama, we gonna live in a big, nice house like the white folks."

He said it quietly, yet I shrunk down in my seat as if one of the white folks passing by had heard him.

I couldn't even address the gravity of what he said without considering that we had just moved from Lake Oswego, Oregon, (ironically called "Lake NoNegro") back to the southside of Chicago. He'd seen a wealthy neighborhood that was filled mostly with white people and an impoverished neighborhood filled with Black people. I had to explain to him right there that there were so many Black people who were wealthy and lived in big houses. I even worked with some of them. I made it a point that day that I would take my son to some of my colleagues' homes when the opportunity arose. Even while we were going through the situation of waiting on a place to live (I learned to say it like that rather than saying we were homeless), I wanted him to see wealth to counter the temporary lack that we were experiencing.

Weeks after leaving the hotel, I was preparing to move into an apartment that my colleague helped me find. People that couldn't help me at all had the most to say when I said I was moving to Englewood. I remained positive and said, "Good things grow in Englewood too!" I asked God to help me see the long-term rewards in spite of the short-term sacrifices. I often had to remind myself that there was purpose even in the pain of the process. I kept pushing forward.

I thought about the letter I wrote to the hotel and wondered why no one had reached out and said anything, not even about the job I'd applied for. Something told me to ask Jazmine, the social worker from the organization who coordinated our stay, if the letter I provided was sent to the hotel. I knew that the letter was so well written and articulately expressed that if it had been received someone would have been impressed enough to respond. Jazmine was meek and mild-mannered and although I was humble, I certainly wasn't mild mannered or timid by far. But I asked her in my most gentle voice, "Jazmine, I haven't heard anything at all back from the hotel and was wondering did you give them the thank you letter that I wrote and sent." She hesitated and nervously said, "No ... well we altered it and sent a slightly different version that was shorter."

There was a long pause. I felt so angry. I took a deep breath and said, "So my signature was at the bottom of what I sent and you saw fit to alter my statement and my story without my consent. You wouldn't have even told me had I not asked." With tears in my eyes, I went on, "You do not get to tell my story the way you want to. THIS IS STILL MY STORY! This is more awful than you have sense enough to even realize. No wonder my son got a basketball and a Gameboy, instead of paid tutoring and educational toys. You chose for me and signed my name to something! I feel violated and voiceless." The young lady didn't know what to say. I guess she was thinking "the audacity of this homeless broad!"

In my Granny's voice, I heard, "You sho' got a lotta nerve!" It wasn't nerve; it was heart. I didn't have much at all, but I had my voice and my story and it was mine to tell!

Christmas was quickly approaching. A friend from high school drove me around the city collecting gifts from seven different organizations. We had the whole car and trunk filled with gifts. We had enough for my son and her two boys and decided to pass out the gifts to people we knew were having a hard time. I didn't know at the time but my friend was preparing for brain surgery. Despite both of our individual struggles, we both still found joy in giving and serving. I was down, but I wasn't out! I was determined to overcompensate in every other way so that my son wouldn't "feel" homeless and would continue to think that we were in "camp."

After the holiday season, we spent a few weeks at hotels downtown on a friend of the family's discount until it was finally time for me to move in. It was probably, no it was definitely, the worst apartment I'd ever had and a far cry from the life of luxury in bland Lake Oswego, but it was a stepping-stone. The inside of the apartment was actually nicer than the exterior so I was going to decorate it and make it nice for us and that I did, all on thrift store dollars! One thing I know for sure is how to find a deal.

It was all good until about four months before my lease was set to expire. One day the janitor started asking us to give him the rent money. Soon maintenance seemed few and far in between, and folks started hanging out in the hallway leaving beer bottles behind. I was grateful that the Lord had given me another temporary stepping-stone, but I'd asked if it could just be for one year and it was getting closer and closer to that deadline. I wasn't claiming that address. I didn't even get my mail sent there. For months I would tithe and write on the address line: "God is building it." I gave every Sunday, even when it was only change. One time I remember only having two quarters in my pocket, which reminded me of the Biblical story of the two mites. I put one in my son's envelope and one in my envelope. I remember having to find an ATM that withdrew in increments of $10 because I only had $20 and it wasn't enough to cover the ATM fee. I needed a way out and a way up!

I was starting to feel trapped and the next thing you know I needed a mouse trap! Enter stage right my knight in shining armor (the co-parent) who gave me a lesson in *How to Catch A Mouse 101*, telling me to go get Tootsie Rolls and traps and he'd come over like superman and save us from the rodents in town. This was no *Tom and Jerry*; I was scared as hell! The very next morning I woke up to a dead mouse on the trap. It turns out Tootsie Rolls work. I called him crying hysterically asking if he could come back and be the mice undertaker. He obliged my request and came to pick up the remains, walking in with his chest sticking out like he had done something ... all the while I was looking upside his bald head wondering why this was even a thing. I wondered, did he have a secret spouse ... could that be why he left my baby in the mouse house? Either way I had to scurry in a hurry! It's funny how I can even laugh writing this when I remember standing up on my couch crying to God, pleading that the mouse would go back into hiding. I was surely hoping that God would reveal His plan sooner rather than later.

While we were waiting for the housing opportunity of our dreams to stop mousing around, we only went there to sleep at night. I had long stopped cooking and eating there. I learned how to cook a whole meal by microwave at one of the fancy grocery stores up north that had an area where I could work while my son ate. The day I got a call about our new place, we were in a restaurant and I was thinking to myself, "I really miss cooking in my own kitchen. I hope this is over soon."

Within a minute of that thought, I saw a call from an unfamiliar number. I answered anticipating a bill collector. Instead the lady said, "Ms. Thompson, are you still looking for an apartment?" I excitedly said, "Yes, but you not calling from Parkway are you?" Slightly confused, she said, "No ma'am." After a slight pause, she went on to say, "We have a new development opening soon and we are wondering if you'd like to proceed with an application." I immediately said, "Yes, how soon can I come in?" She said, "How about the day after tomorrow?" Without hesitation, I said, "I'll take it!" I think I did a solo soul train line right there in that restaurant!

My joy was short-lived because soon after applying I received a rejection letter in the mail. Apparently, the furniture items I had left behind in Portland, and the burn mark on the carpet from my son's escapade with fire, had left me with a sizeable bill that showed up on my credit report. I'll never forget how defeated I felt standing in my Grandmother's kitchen reading that letter. For the first time, I finally felt like the homeless b%^&* they'd been calling me. I cried and then I prayed. I knew it was the place for me. It was in a great neighborhood with better schools and three libraries within walking distance, one literally steps away. I did not want to accept that I had come so close to home only to have the door slammed in my face. I asked God to turn my rejection into an acceptance and if in fact it wasn't for me to allow me to let it go and accept that He had something else in mind.

In the meantime, I kept calling and explaining my situation and asking for an appeal. The head lady was nonchalant and slightly mean. She said, "Ms. Thompson, calling every three days is not going to help. You just have to wait. There is nothing more we can do." As crazy as it sounds, I went over to the building and walked around the neighborhood praying that somehow God would make this place our new home. I felt that if I walked the grounds, praying with each stride, God would bless my steps. ("The steps of a good man are ordered by the LORD: and he delighteth in his way." Psalm 37:23).

The next week I called and the mean manager was no longer there. The new manager seemed to be much more willing to help. I pleaded my case to her as quickly as I could, telling her that the bill showing was not from unpaid rent but from furniture I had to leave behind when I left due to extenuating circumstances. She said, "Bring me any supporting documentation you have and we're gonna figure this out."

I went in the next morning with my file folder in hand ready to plead my case. It turned out I didn't need to as she already had my lease drawn up and my keys in hand. She pointed to where I needed to sign and with tears in my eyes I said quietly, "This is the lease." She said, "Yes, I received an email about you. Someone spoke highly of you." I was so thankful that I didn't have words. I just thought how God had advocated for me when I'd run out of ways to fight for myself. The leasing agent's voice brought me back. He said, "Ms. Thompson, we can go do the walkthrough so you can see your new place." As we rode up in the elevator, he said, "You're on the top floor ... on the side with a great view." I almost held my breath the whole way up.

We got off the elevator to the smell of new carpet. I thought to myself, "God really was building it!" This was a brand spanking new building! With difficulty, I held back my tears. He turned the locks and I still can't describe how grateful I felt in that moment. I walked over to the floor-to-ceiling windows and glanced out straight ahead to a cathedral church with crosses on both sides. Just then, the church bell started to ring. I looked over to the east and there it was ... my wish from the hotel window ... to live in a place that had a view of downtown. I could see the Sears Tower. God had honored all of my requests. I felt so full. Like the ol' folks down south used to say, I couldn't hold my peace. I let out a Baptist praise right there in front of the leasing agent.

After I left with my keys, I decided to walk over to that church I could see out of my window. I just wanted to sit on the steps and give God praise. To my surprise, that church was Notre Dame of Chicago. My mouth flew open. God sure has a sense of humor. I couldn't afford to go to Notre Dame, but instead Notre Dame came to me.

That 4th of July I celebrated MY independence from insecurity, disconnection from doubt and freedom from fear. Last year I'd told my son the gunshots were fireworks. This year we saw the fireworks shooting over the downtown skyline right from our living room window. In that moment, I felt like we finally had something worth celebrating.

## Connection Clue

When was the last time you were fully willing to go through the fire for a set period of time to cause an infinite outpouring of blessings? It's a selfless sacrifice. You see, the blessings are often not just for you.

In some parts of the world there are fire-activated seeds, one being the seeds of the eucalyptus. Their seeds can only open after they have physically gone through a fire and that is the only way they can reproduce and produce! You see to activate something and set it in motion, there has to be a catalyst. The thing you see as a crisis could actually be the catalyst that leads to your blessing!

At one point, I felt that my situation was a hindrance to my success. The enemy taunted me that my circumstances were evidence that it would not work together for my good and that all my efforts were in vain. That is when I finally cried. I wanted to lay down. I felt like my legs would give out. In that moment, as dramatic as it was powerful, God said,

"Stand UP and give in to MY will." My retort was, "How can this be Your will for me God? You said abundance; I am in lack." God told me, "It is in your *temporary* lack that I will unleash the abundance of your inheritance. This discomfort that you feel, this lack that you speak of, is preparation for the surplus. Do you not think that I can use this too?"

You will lose some things along the way, material items, close friends, and maybe even some family too. Sometimes you lose, not in the physical, as the thing is still present but has no presence. But in all thy losing, know that God can and will turn the loss into a gain. Whatever you may lose along the way, don't harden your heart. Forgive those who kicked you while you were down. They may be undeserving of your forgiveness according to your feelings and their transgressions, but you deserve to live as if you've never ever been hurt.

So whatever you lose along the way, don't lose your faith. It is the substance of things unseen and the light in the tunnel when darkness is unveiled all around you. It is in darkness where the seed first takes root. It is also in darkness that God's light shines brightest. Where is the light in your dark situation? How do you expand that light?

Stay connected to the source and ask Him (in His infinite wisdom) to give you increased discernment and wisdom while orchestrating a village of people who will make contact with you and use their light to illuminate yours. This is how faith in action starts to serve as a catalyst for things to line up in a powerful way. As you experience a shift to elevate you, you will not only change your circumstances. but you'll change your life.

## Connection Clue Bonus

What is something that you have been struggling with—something that is painful, but going through it gave you perspective? What teachable moments, solutions, and breakthrough stories can help you navigate other challenges as well as impacting and inspiring others?

**Audacity Affirmation**

Everything I need is within my reach. If I don't possess it within me, I am attracting it to me by operation of my gifts in service to others. No good thing will be withheld from me. The financial means to achieve my goals is coming to me as if I am magnetically charged, because I am AUDACIOUS!

# Chapter 7

# Overcoming Injustice

Blessed is the man that endureth temptation: for when he is tried, he shall receive the crown of life, which the Lord hath promised to them that love him.
James 1:12

**"I'm no longer accepting the things I cannot change ... I'm changing the things I cannot accept."—Dr. Angela Davis**

Courtrooms and hospitals are two places that I know for sure really bad, life-changing stuff happens. Hospitals don't make me think about lollipops and stickers, but more about the fear that came from skewed perspectives piercing cold like daggers and icicles during Chicago's coldest winter ever. I knew winter and I knew why she was so cold.

I thought lack of knowledge would get you taken advantage of, like having the information would somehow bulletproof you from the snares of the system. I learned the hard way that knowing (and saying that you know) makes you that much more of a target—a target to be silenced through discretionary policies that bend towards bias more so than fairness on the scales of justice. Often you are subjected to abuses of power that breed distrust for the system. To add insult to injury, if you stand up for yourself as a Black woman, you're dismissed and labeled as an angry Black woman, which somehow invalidates your pain because you really don't get a right to emotion. Crying is a weakness. Gotta be tough. Stay strong. Don't let 'em see you sweat. And my favorite: can't keep a good woman down.

My favorite line in one of my all-time favorite movies is when Ms. Sofia said that famous line in *The Color Purple* ... seven words that seemed to sum it all up for me ... "All my life I had to fight." Not only did I come out fighting, my son did too! He was born with his umbilical cord around his neck. I cried and held my breath waiting to hear him cry. There were five people in the room. My Godmother cut his cord after his father declined saying he was too scared. A room full of people and I still felt like it was just me and my little baby. That's how it started and many nights and days that's how it felt and often that's exactly how it was.

I've had my biggest fights in advocating as a single mother. I remember Fantasia's song "Baby Mama" saying: "It's like a badge of honor to be a baby mama." Well, people try to treat you like it's a badge of shame. I vividly remember realizing how a mother without the father in front of or at her side leaves the mother as an open target for all forms of predators that mistake her for prey. It's a tragedy that mama bear always has to be on the defense.

Once you see, you cannot unsee how easy it is for our families to fall to the ruins of a lost legacy. Our children can easily become part of a mill that tells them to accumulate debt and work for people who invest in the demise of their people. You can never unsee the pain that is a direct result of injustice.

I couldn't afford for my son to go to private school again so I volunteered at a couple in order to get him positioned to possibly get the same scholarship that allowed me to attend private school, I quickly saw the difference in parent choice and involvement. There was no us versus them culture. However, when you are paying for something, it entitles you to the benefits that those receiving it for free are denied of daily. **There is indeed a cost to free.** Public benefits, public housing, public school, all potentially the bare minimum, give less choice and protections and more restrictions. Even going to the hospital and the experience you have there is very much predicated on how one presents yourself and the color of your skin. Yes, that is a fact, more than one would publicly like to admit. Here's a synopsis of a few experiences to let you know just how merciless a hospital really can be.

In the early stages of my pregnancy, I still had public aid medical insurance. I was in the process of being interviewed for a management role that included full benefits and a company vehicle. I was looking to have my baby at one of the best hospitals in the city, not the public hospital where I was born. I called and asked for the doctor that my cousin's mother said was the best. I got up to the insurance question in the first few minutes of the intake call for an appointment and it turned out neither that doctor nor the hospital were taking any more public aid patients at the time. Almost emphatically, she repeated, “We’re not accepting that insurance as a method of payment.” I called the second best hospital in the city and they told me to go to their clinic location after I disclosed my insurance.

A couple weeks later I found out that I got the job. As soon as my medical benefits kicked in, I drove my company car to the doctor’s office and parked in the garage. I went in and said, “Hi Marisol, my name is Andrea Thompson. I spoke with you regarding an appointment and I know you said that you weren’t taking public aid patients at the time, but since I am not a public aid patient anymore, I wanted to come down here in person and present you with my insurance card to see if I can get an appointment now.” Marisol turned a little red, but she tried her best to act unbothered. I said it as nicely as I could, yet it didn’t take the sting out of it and she apparently felt my disdain. I got an appointment that same day.

As I left, for the first time, I wondered why there were so many Black-owned funeral homes, but I only ever heard of one Black-owned hospital. We can bury, but we can’t birth? We can bury, but we can’t help each other heal? The devil is a lie!

So now that we have seen just a glimpse of how insurance matters, let's go to this other elitist hospital's behind the scenes experience. I was working one of the biggest parades in the country, the famous Bud Billiken Day Parade. I had a headache and felt weak, yet I told myself to persist. I had worked this parade for the last three years and had fond memories of attending as a kid. Between the skates, snowballs, and nachos, man those were the days! I always wanted to dance down King Drive in the parade but my Mama said, "You can pay to dance down the street in the hot sun and make your asthma act up, or you can sit in the shade and help me sell nachos and make you some money." When she put it like that, selling nachos definitely seemed like a much better choice.

I counted it an honor to have my small business be an ambassador for a parade with so much historical context right in the community where I grew up. Proudly displaying my media pass, I had arrived at the politicians' breakfast that morning. I started doing interviews and the flash from a camera made me feel slightly dizzy. I knew then that something was off, but I ate some fruit, drank some water and convinced myself that it was just a headache and that I needed to push through. We always tell ourselves to press on when we really need a time out. Sometimes persisting just means taking a temporary break to recharge, but I didn't take heed of the need to slow down my speed.

We started walking down the famous Dr. Martin Luther King Jr. Drive. (It was previously known as Grand Boulevard, then South Park Way, before it was renamed in 1968.) When I made it to 49th Street, I saw my son on the sidelines of the parade with my family. As he hugged my neck, I felt a sharp pain. I knew then I might not make it to the parade after party. I walked another block looking for my media team. The sharp pains hit again. I stopped one of the Dusable Museum buses and asked to get on because I was feeling weak. He said, "It's a liability to have you on board with us." I said, "Sir, I am out here working with a press pass on and I am telling you I believe I am having a medical emergency and that's all you can say? Okay." I started to walk off and I guess I looked sick because he called me back and said, "Come on."

After I sat down on the bus, I looked around and saw memorabilia all around me. Photos of my ancestors in protests. Photos that demonstrated sheer strength in the midst of adversity. I tried to sit up with my back straight and my head held up high, but I could no longer ignore the pain I felt in my neck that seemed to be radiating to my head. I laid back, unable to sit up any longer. The driver said, "You can't sleep on the bus!" I said, "Sir, tell me when you get to 51st Street so I can get off and walk to Provident Hospital."

Somehow I got to the hospital a half block off the parade route. When I got in, I immediately knew without a doubt that it wasn't the place to get treatment but the place to get ... treated like you weren't valued or important ... and treated like a second class citizen that should wait and just be grateful. After 30 minutes, I left to try to find my way to University Hospital. I flagged down a car with a woman I didn't even know because I couldn't even get a RideShare (the Lyft and Uber of the day) pickup due to the street closures. I asked if she could drive me three blocks down to where my family was because I was sick and couldn't even walk. She said, "Come on, get in!" I thanked her and got out seemingly as quickly as I got in.

Everything was spinning and I could barely walk straight. I saw my Grandmother's pickup truck parked at the end of the corner. I got in the bed of the truck and stretched out. I dialed a family member and uttered the words, "I'm real sick. Somebody come get me to the university." I heard someone tell somebody else and I passed out. I woke up to someone on the phone saying they were taking me to the hospital. I said, "Please don't tell anyone else. I don't want to cause alarm. My work team doesn't even know." I wasn't in the hospital an hour before I started to get texts from colleagues and a couple clients saying they hoped I was okay. I wondered how they knew. Later I found out that the same person who took me to the hospital had posted to social media asking for prayers for me because I was rushed from the parade to the hospital by ambulance. I came in as discretely as possible via pickup truck only to get let down by someone I trusted. Folks will publicize your pain without any comprehension of the impact of the news they are sharing.

You have to watch where you place people in your auditorium because everybody isn't equipped to have a front row seat. Think about the flight attendant's announcement about the emergency row. "If you are not able or willing to perform the tasks associated with the position in the event of an emergency, please alert an attendant so that she can reseat you."

Who do you need to reseat? Indeed, you may actually need for some people to be deplaned. Write it down to make it plain (or plane)!

| Reseat | Deplane |
|---|---|
| | |
| | |
| | |
| | |
| | |
| | |
| | |
| | |
| | |

## Critical Position: Resiliency is a Mutha

Sitting in the hospital sicker than I'd ever been, I was praying that whatever was wrong with me wouldn't cause me to have to sit on the sidelines for too long. I couldn't think about my pain or healing because all I could think about was meetings and moments that I would miss that could position me to advance my business. A couple hours later, I was still in the waiting room in a wheelchair, with increasingly unbearable pain. During this chaos, a family member walked in with my son in hand saying that she had to leave him there with me while she dropped everyone off. I couldn't understand how it made sense for her to bring my son to a hospital where I was sick saying there was nowhere else to take him. I said, "I only asked you to take him to my Grandma. What is going on?" I was in too much pain to try to reconcile the foolishness of it all. It made no sense. I could barely hold my head up, so I simply said, "Okay." I handed my son the phone and asked him to sit in the chair next to me with his feet on mine so I could feel if he moved.

Hours later we'd finally made it to the back, but they didn't have a room so they put me on a stretcher in the hallway. They couldn't even offer me a room, just a stretcher in the hallway, after hours of being in a chair in the waiting room. I was in excruciating pain by then. The lights seemed to make my head hurt worse. They gave me some pain meds. By that time, I knew something was really wrong. A nurse came to me and said, "We think you have an infection that is attacking your nervous system. We're going to have to extract fluid from your spine and need you to sign some paperwork in the event that things don't go as planned." The phrase, "Don't go as planned" echoed in my mind. It was like her words were coming out in slow motion.

Reality intruded through the pain. What about my insurance? I knew I didn't have enough life insurance and only had public aid medical coverage. What about my son? I'd been calling the family member that dropped him off for hours, literally hours. The hospital was calling. I was calling. No answer. No response. I knew from years of experience that calling my son's Dad, even from a hospital, wouldn't necessarily mean he was coming, but I called and texted anyway. I told him we were at the hospital. He finally responded with, "I'll pray for you." I wrote, "I need you to get Jeremiah." I didn't hear from him again until days later.

A social worker came to my bedside saying, "Ma'am. Excuse me. You need to wake up. If you don't have anyone to come get your child, we're going to have to call DCFS." As weak as I was, I managed to lift my head up. It was the dreaded acronym I'd heard all my life. "Hold on, say what ... why. I am here with my son. I am sick." She said, "He can't be here by himself" as if I were invisible. I said, "I am right here with him. He is right here on the bed in the hallway with me sitting on my feet." I couldn't contain my anger. I didn't even get the right to be sick. No one was coming for me and my son. No one.

I said, "Ma'am, don't you come by me for the duration of my stay or I'm going to holler like you're trying to kill me. Don't you dare show your pale, wrinkled face by my bedside, not even once more. You have no empathy and no bedside manner so don't you dare show up on the side of my bed anymore!" With that, I couldn't keep my head up another second. I dropped back down to the pillow which cushioned my head and hid my tears. No one cared enough to help. How many times had a mother come to the hospital with her baby and been told some mess like that simply because she didn't have anyone to come get the baby. That sickened me even worse than I already was.

Before I could shed another tear, a young lady, a Black nurse, came to me with so much empathy in her voice. She said, "Ma'am, I can take him to the cafeteria with your consent, but they have to do the extraction procedure within the next 30 minutes because the pain you feel at the base of your neck means you're at risk for nerve damage. We have to move swiftly even under these circumstances." She added, "The social worker didn't have to talk to you like that. It was very insensitive, but if you allow me to, I'll help you as best I can." I thanked her and said I'd consent.

In every situation there is a ram in the bush or rather an angel in the midst. I felt horrible though. How could I have chosen to nearly lose my life giving birth to a child by a man who would only send a text saying he'd pray for me instead of coming to get our son. Our relationship was awful when we were together and was possibly worse as co-parents. I was convinced that I'd had a baby by a mean man who hated me, seemingly the next inappropriate sequel to the first man I'd known, my mean Daddy. Nevertheless, I had no time for woe is me. I had to be a strong Black woman even in the midst of being in the most excruciating pain because I had no man-made covering. Even still, I was kept—kept by God—and I was in His hands. In spite of my mistakes and iniquities, even with the out-of-wedlock scarlet letter, God still had a plan.

Just as the woman was taking my son out of the room, the nurse leaned over and said, "We think you have meningitis. It's good that you came in when you did." My eyes widened. She said, "If you had gone home to rest, it's possible that you may not have awakened. This is serious." My wide eyes started to water.

It was just before midnight. As I looked at the clock, I thought about the song, "In the Midnight Cry" and in my spirit, I called, "God help me!" For the first time in my life, I thought about wanting to live for ME. I mean since being post-partum, I had really only seen my life as worth living because of my son, but in that moment I realized more than ever that God has a calling on my life and the enemy was working overtime to stop it so I figured it must be great.

I thought about how God saved me in the womb. I said, "God save me to fulfil your purpose. I want to do everything you put in me to benefit my son, the sons of your son, and the daughters that are apples of your eyes like me. People are hurting Lord. Heal me so that I may serve as a testament to relentless faith and your saving grace. God save me, heal me, and make me whole. I am not alone, for you are with me." I wanted to toughen up after the prayer, you know, wipe my tears away, straighten up my crown and put back on my cape, but in that moment I decided I would just be still. The crown needed to rest and the cape needed to be pressed.

I'm not going to lie that I felt slightly stressed when I saw the needle on the table. The nurse said, "I'll give you a couple minutes to get settled because the most important thing is that you clear your mind and be completely still. I took that as confirmation. Be still.

Just then a family member stormed in the door with a ready lie, "I had to feed all the policeses at the parade and get all my grills back to the house plus drop off 10 kids 'cause every year I sell food at the parade and I give the policeses free food." Those two times that she made police plural made me feel sicker. I wanted to say, "Lady I been here sick as a dog with my son for over five hours, been told to sign paperwork in case I die, and been threatened by a social worker less than two hours ago!" I wanted to scream, "Just get my son and take him to my Grandma's house before you make my head hurt more." Instead, I said something next, and I still can't understand why I said it. I guess in that moment I just wanted to confide in her. I don't know how I forgot that she was the biggest newspaper on this side of the Mississippi Delta. I told her, "They think it's meningitis." She looked at me and said, "Uhhhh, who you got busy with and caught that from?" I looked ashamed before looking at the nurse like, "Can you believe this? This is how she is." The nurse shook her head, looking at me like, "That's okay. I've seen worse!" before telling her, "Ma'am, this is an airborne virus not an STD."

I wanted to tell my family member to "hurry up and leave" like that corner store cashier in the movie *Menace II Society*, but I was in pain and I didn't wanna raise no Cain. I just prayed that God would let me be still because in that moment I realized I didn't have enough life insurance nor a strong executor of my little estate. Quite simply, I couldn't afford to die yet, and I had to make more money to afford to live. Fortunately, the Lord heard my midnight cry and I lived to fight another day.

## Code Black

With his final breaths, George Floyd called for his mama. On May 25, 2020, we all watched what many of us had seen, known about and experienced personally more times than we could bear to express. The utter and blatant disrespect of Black folks at the hands of police who intend to serve injustice ice cold and protect the code blue was there for all to see.

Black folks need a code. A code to specify where to go to when things go awry, as they often do. A code to record when we see racist police rearing their ugly heads. A code to pursue justice with assigned counsellors of law. Let me make this last part plain. It has always annoyed me how the media is able to go onto a crime scene with the red tape still there and record a mother at this extremely painful time of her life and display it for the whole world to view before her child is even out of the ambulance. I was tired of seeing Black mothers screaming ... and crying. The most terrible cry I have ever heard is the one of a mother whose child is snatched away violently. It isn't that she doesn't deserve to have her cries heard by the people, but it doesn't need to be broadcasted in front of the whole world so insensitively.

Other cultures have a representative: a family member, a friend or a lawyer designated to speak on the family's behalf to cover the mother, giving her the respect to grieve privately. Often the respect of privacy isn't granted to grieving Black mothers. There is no shroud and there is no shield. For that matter, I have literally seen young sons and daughters laid out on the pavement for hours. Even more concerning is the fact that the right representation to handle the case only appears out of nowhere when the victim is killed. So only in death does justice somehow show itself and sometimes not even then.

## Overcoming the Code Blue Betrayal

A false witness shall not be unpunished,
and he that speaketh lies shall not escape.
Proverbs 19:5

I learned early on that serving and protecting was no more than a baseless slogan written on the side of Chicago police cars as they drove away with handcuffed suspects, sometimes innocent, but almost always Black and brown faces to be served by overworked public defenders. And, yes, hold on to your hard hats as I'm just getting started!

First off, let me say I grew up only seeing the police do bad things, most times to good people. I saw situations get worse just because people called the police for help. I didn't fear the police. In fact I was taught not to. "Don't mess with the pigs, and I ain't just talking about swine food" my Muslim Uncle would say. It's a vulgarity and I felt bad saying it because a couple, just a couple, of people I love and grew up with became officers. I saw a need for police, but nevertheless I couldn't ignore or unsee the things I had seen that would yield me to understand my Uncle's disposition and distrust of what we had come to see as a legal gang.

Two of my earliest memories of police interactions were when I had an officer play "Officer Friendly" with me and then took me to a hospital. I only saw my parents one time and that was through the small basement-sized window that showed just a glimpse of outside. They peered in ... waving. I was probably only five, but I distinctly remember climbing out of the bed with the high rails one night and sneaking down to the phone at the nurses' station. I picked it up, but of course I didn't know what to do after that.

"If you'd like to make a call, please hang up and ..."

"Call my grandma," I said.

The recorded operator kept talking.

I said, "Call my grandma please!"

The next interaction that stands out amongst all the others is when one of my cousin's friends was killed after the police attempted to pull him over. We saw him get out of the car and run, but he didn't make it far before we saw him fall. He was hit with two shots in the back, one through the heart. The police surrounded him and told everyone to stay back. When the police circle dissolved, there was a gun next to his body. He never tried to shoot and was shot in the back while running away, but it didn't matter what we saw or what really actually happened for that matter. Like Officer Fine (nicknamed that by the block girls because of his resemblance to Morris Chestnut) told me, "There's a thousand laws on the books and at any point and time we can pick one as a reason to lock you up."

Officer Fine had been to my house more times than I could count, for one reason or another, and he had a nickname for me: "Smart Trouble." Every time he'd say it, I'd say, "Officer, my name is Andrea," but he didn't pay me any mind. He said, "You're going to learn the hard way that the law is always right, even when it's not on your side." I looked at him like he was speaking Chinese. The law was definitely not always right from where I stood. In fact, it was dead wrong and torturously unfair. Jon Burge and Chicago's legacy of police torture, as the *Chicago Tribune* called it, fueled my desire to understand the law and be a voice for innocent people. I felt like it was my duty to expose and prosecute bad police officers because I knew that if people saw just a little bit of the little I saw they would be astounded by how people are dehumanized when a police officer abuses their power with lack of regard and often sheer hatred.

Even reaching for your phone can be deadly, especially without following a strict set of precautions to give advance announcement of what you're reaching for. Assuming you live through that, you could get arrested simply because they don't want you to record. If you're lucky, you will be allowed to record the injustice and hope they have the conscience to do the right thing rather than slip through or create some legal reasons to justify what is clearly wrong in plain view of the nation's face.

Code blue often denies justice for Black and brown people, choosing to be judge and jury. With the pandemic on top of the epidemic of brown and Black voices being permanently silenced, I just couldn't watch anymore of the videos. I avoided the news for just a slight sense of peace even if it caused me to temporarily deflect from the harsh realities of looting, shootings and even more sorrowful things.

However, something on my timeline that chilled my blood caused me to stop because this one man was calling out for his mother. An officer was kneeling on his neck, so very casually, with his hands in his pocket. It was happening again, in full view of eyewitnesses and the eyes of the world. The man said he couldn't breathe. A man yelled out, "Hey, that's a blood choke; you're killing him. Let him breathe." A young girl recorded it on her phone too, pleading for the officer to get off of him. He didn't budge. Chauvin knelt on George Floyd's neck for more than 8 minutes.

Eight minutes. And 46 seconds.

It wasn't the first time, by far, but for many it was the last straw. We don't even get to deal with the impact of one loss before someone else becomes the next hashtag.

I thought about my son and "the talk" we would have when he got closer to Tamir Rice's age. My son said that he was scared of the police, and as much as I wanted to tell him not to fear any man for God is with him, I knew that while under God we are created equal, that is not the case under the knee of the law. Quite frankly, my son has the right to be scared considering the constant stream of stories. The truth be told, I am scared for him.

I thought that moving to a good neighborhood with good schools, or working hard to send him to private school would help us to be less exposed to racism. However, I had to learn that while financial security gives you the means to fight back, it doesn't mean you won't have to fight. You can see racism in the projects and in penthouses too. People can see your Black skin as a weapon wherever you are. Oh, and please don't dare be confident and firm in your speech, respectful but not timid, as then you're an angry Black woman. One of my mentors once told me, "Andrea, as a Black woman in business, you're either going to be a pushover or a bitch; you'd rather be the latter." I was young and half-jokingly I said, "What if I don't want to be either?" I think a smirk was the only response I got. The fact of the matter is, when you're assertive, know the policies and have the audacity to stand up for yourself, people in high positions can sometimes see your stance as demeaning to them and their intimidation leads to an abuse of power. I really feel that the motive behind so much egregious and blatant racism is because Black folks standing tall makes some people feel small.

I'll never forget my colleague that got me an interview at a hotel briefing me by saying, "You have to tone down that Black Lives Matter stuff if they transfer you here." He went on to tell me how he had to adjust in order to get promoted. I asked exactly what he meant and he explained that he wore glasses to seem more intelligent, and not only did he code switch, he made sure not to appear too friendly with other Black people. He then made the most shocking statement of them all, "When I talk to white men, I usually take a seat because by me being tall, I never want them to have to look up to me because it makes me seem intimidating." I knew right then, for sure, that he'd never come out of the friend zone.

A lil' old lady once told me, "I don't wanna keep up no mess and I don't mean to bother nobody, but I know you got to stand for something or you'll fall for anything. Stand firm on the buckle of truth and don't take no wooden nickels." Amen! We gotta press on, and get in good trouble. We gotta fight the good fight and keep the faith, especially in the midst of overcoming injustice. In short, we must be audacious!

## Connection Clue

Speaking out can make you a target. Has there been a time when you've had to make a difficult choice, keeping the greater good in mind?

How have you continued to love and forgive in spite of the hurt and hate?

**Audacity Affirmation**

I resolve to speak truth to power even when it's uncomfortable. The truth I have the courage to speak will free generations to come. My voice matters and my truth matters even when wickedness in high places seeks to suppress my words. The truth is my loudspeaker exists in a world that is sometimes tone deaf to truth. I embody the audacity to STILL rise and to STILL speak out!

# Chapter 8

## Meeting Michelle Obama (Yes THE Mrs. Michelle Robinson Obama)!

My Lord, this is a book in and of itself. I've published some of this as an article in a local newspaper and even created a blog to convey the experience, and still I didn't do it justice so I decided to convey in my first book how THE Forever FLOTUS was a plug for me.

This is a little embarrassing, but I'm just getting started so here goes. When I first heard the then Senator Barack Obama speaking on stage at the Blues Festival on 47$^{th}$ Street, then Alderman Dorothy Tillman rocking her stylish, signature, church boss lady hat introduced him and I started wondering what he had to say. Could he relate to us? Where was he from? I remember Betty O, one of my neighborhood aunties saying, "He's cute" and a slightly inebriated woman responding, "He probably got a white wife."

I remember thinking to myself, "Yeah, a man that educated and accomplished probably did get a white woman from the suburbs. Girls like me don't get that lucky." My subconscious continued, "I bet she looks like Vanessa Williams: good hair, light skin, and a nice pointy nose like my Southern Grandma would say. Yep, she must be because nappy-headed, dark-skinned girls didn't get men like him to love them like that." Boy was I wrong and foolish, but these thoughts came from somewhere.

I wasn't a little girl like Parker, but inside me was the little girl who had been told in more ways than one—in many places and familiar spaces—that my skin tone, hair texture, urban dialect and wide nose made me somehow less desirable, but having a nice shape helped me to balance out my faults. I was taught somewhere that men were more interested in the shape of my body than the landscape of my mind. I'm so glad I finally learned to love me, all of me, just the way God made me. That's why I didn't get that nose job 'cause I didn't know how to explain it to young girls who need to know they are beautiful ... just as they are.

Rewinding, I actually shed a few tears when I learned that the then Senator Obama's wife was Michelle Robinson Obama, born and raised on the southside of Chicago. I remember seeing her on TV for the first time. I kept murmuring, "She's like me, her hair ... she's pretty ... just like me." I said the last part softly and bashfully. I still stand in awe of Michelle. I needed to see women like her where she was, holding it together and doing better! I needed to see me in a woman where Michelle was.

I wonder how many other little girls, and even grown women, saw themselves in Mother ... Sister ... Michelle. I mean no disrespect by calling her that, but what do you call someone who has inspired you, and made it to the White House, and did it so gracefully. Hopefully, Forever FLOTUS will suffice.

## Taking Action to Create Change Now

After learning more about the Obamas, I felt even more compelled to get involved. My family has always emphasized the importance of political involvement and how difficult our forefathers and foremothers fought for the right to vote. Detractors said he wasn't Black enough, and that his name was too difficult to pronounce. I wanted him to win to prove their thoughts and judgments to be wrong. But more to the point, if he could make it to the White House, there was more hope for me than I previously knew.

My Grandmother made her famous turkey chili and my Auntie who knew how to make a dollar holla like a flea market superstar came up with the idea to give the chili away to encourage people to register to vote. We would also sell Obama t-shirts to donate to his campaign and fund our trips to other states where we would canvass for him. We volunteered in Ohio, Indiana and Wisconsin.

We started across the street from Pappy's, the neighborhood liquor store that was like the Cheers of the Midwest. We were set up in front of a McDonalds that to my delight was and still is operated by a Black woman. We served over 100 bowls and I left to go to work at the Infiniti Store downtown. It was an odd feeling going from a block filled with so much obvious lack and disparity marked by currency exchanges guised as banks to being a clerk on a showroom floor near the Magnificent Mile where people barely blinked at dropping $20k for a down payment on a brand new car.

Before I could make it a few blocks, I heard gunshots ring out and panicked. I got off the bus and ran back down, calling my Grandma, desperately hoping she'd be able to work the cell phone this time. She cried out, "Don't come back; they shot him! Oh Lord!" The fact that she said "him" let me know that it wasn't her or my Aunt. I felt a temporary moment of relief before I quickly thought about my block brothers and cousins. We knew nearly everybody. Who was "he"? I couldn't run anymore so I stopped and took a break to hit my inhaler. I tried to call my brother and didn't get an answer. My mind went back to high school when I saw my godbrother's body lifeless with gunshot wounds. I was angry that I couldn't run anymore and hurt that I didn't know who he was or if he'd survive. All I could do in that moment was pray.

I finally found out that the "he" was Zeke. Zeke was 19-years-old. He graduated from Dyett High School. He went off to college and got shot and killed in the McDonalds parking lot that day while he was home visiting. My Aunt held him and prayed as he left the world. Just a mile away from Obama's home, this young man was gone. My Aunt cried in a way that pierced our hearts. She'd asked him earlier if he was registered to vote, but the last thing she asked him was if he was saved before praying for him. She couldn't save him, but in those few moments she petitioned God to save him even if he didn't physically make it. That night I heard more gunshots ring out, perhaps in retaliation or maybe another brawl waiting to result in a death. In that moment, I realized how desperately we needed change. We'd grown to love Obama, but we were also fighting for the much-needed change that his campaign echoed.

I got a job offer as a flight attendant that required me to do a six-week training in St. Louis. I took the position and volunteered there too. I was in training so I still got to take another position as an election worker in Chicago. We worked the weeks leading up to the election in a warehouse on the city's westside. I got assigned to a team of older women. They talked about what this election meant to them having experienced the Civil Rights Movement. I grew fond of them. They loved sharing stories from the good ol' days and I enjoyed listening in. I walked into the lunchroom one day expecting to hear them laughing and joking, but instead was met with utter silence and eyes glued to the TV. Violence had hit the doorstep of our Chicago idol, Jennifer Hudson. Two family members were dead and a child was missing! Right there in the lunchroom one of the ladies on my team that we affectionately called Granny G broke out and said, "Let's pray." Some people looked at her strangely, but I immediately went and grabbed her hand and man did she pray a prayer. There wasn't a dry eye in the room afterwards.

On election night, it was surreal. I worked at the polls and when I saw several malfunctions and issues I was certain that some kind of ballot mishandling, Florida-type scenario would steal this opportunity. When Obama won it was electric! I was never so glad to be wrong!

I left the polling place, dropped off my team and blasted Jezzy's "My President's Black" on rotation from my Oak Park base to downtown. When I got downtown, babbbbyyyyyyy, the people were out sharing love like we all had won the lottery. I immediately took out my phone and emailed my manager confirming what I had previously verbally told her, "If Obama wins, I'm gonna need some days off to go to the inauguration." Well, they gave me an ultimatum so I rented a car and picked up my last check in an Obama t-shirt. How's that for audacity?!

Without a ticket, I hit the road for the capital. I was hoping that I could somehow work my volunteer pass. After over 17 hours of driving, including a hailstorm, I made it there. Just as I was leaving from the last gate and was giving up hope, a veteran in a wheelchair told me he'd seen me trying to get in earlier and couldn't catch up with me in the crowd. He said he had a companion pass and to just follow him. I did and we ended up on 3rd Street with a bird's eye view.

I will never forget how proud I felt seeing Michelle Obama wave with that light green suit on. "She's from the southside of Chicago, where I'm from," I said proudly to people I didn't even know while we both smiled and looked. It meant so much more to me than I could muster the words to say. It still does.

While I was in the nation's capital, I found out some interesting family history. To my surprise, my Dad had a sister in Washington, D.C. who was an attorney and graduated from Yale Law to boot. To make matters cooler, her namesake is Dr. Angela Davis. Fortunately, she let me stay with her while I was in D.C. I must have asked her all the questions that lawyers get tired of prospective students asking, but she was gracious enough to give me the rundown. Even though I still felt like a trailblazer, it was comforting to know that someone in my family had already walked on the path I wanted to tread.

## Now the Farewell (8 years later)

At the end of President Obama's term, I got a ticket to the farewell speech. My aunt was rushing me to meet her early. I calmly said, "I won't be razzled; it's going to all work out." But when I arrived and saw the maze of people, I sighed and thought, "At this rate, I'll only be able to see the speech on a little screen from a nosebleed distance." There were over 20 lanes of people and when I got in line, I just didn't feel right. Something said, "Get out of line and go stand around the front." While hovering near the main entryway where the maze started, I saw my old boss. She was the first Black woman-owned business I'd worked for and had held one of the biggest expos at the McCormick Place for over a decade. She was making calls to her people and I knew if she was having trouble I didn't stand a chance.

While I was thinking about going back to the line, I heard an attendant say "accessible entrance." I remembered how I'd gotten into the first inauguration with a man in a wheelchair who had a companion ticket and no one accompanying him. I stood by the entrance looking for someone who I could tell how much I loved the Obamas, hoping that they would let me go in with them. I saw a veteran and quickly reached into my jacket pocket. All I had was airline peanuts and some gum. I said, "Thank you for your service, Sir. You want some gum?" He was obviously in a rush but me offering the gum slowed him down. I walked alongside him and quickly pleaded my case. He said, "I don't know if they will let you in, but you welcome to try."

The security guard said, "Sir, do you have the pass that came with your ticket? He said, "I don't know nothing, but I'm here to see Obama. Let us in!" and he took off like he was in a motorized chair. I looked at the gatekeeper and said, "He's so excited. I'm trying to keep him calm, but if I don't catch up with him no telling what damage my po' client could do." The man smirked and said, "Go 'head."

I caught up with my wing man and he said, "I didn't know which way it would go, but I played the role and was hoping that would work for you." I laughed and told him my name and he told me his was Paul. We went a long way to a door that put us so close to the stage that I started taking pictures. I couldn't believe I had made it so close. I was beyond thankful. My ticket was general yet I still made it to VIP! I looked at Paul with so much excitement that I had tears in my eyes. He looked at me with a stern face and said, "Andrea with your charm and talk, I think we can get closer." I gave him a look like, "What you talkin' 'bout Willis?" He said, "I think we are supposed to be even closer Andrea, so let's just try and see."

While I only half-heartedly believed that we could get closer, I took the brake off his wheelchair and pushed us back through the entry point we'd just come in from and down the ramp towards the VIP area. Once we made it there, I sat and watched and strategized about how we could get in without the yellow-colored tickets that were required for that area. I tried talking to the lady taking tickets but she was unmoved by my pleas: "NO Ticket, NO VIP." I'd already made it two checkpoints past the general admission ticket so I was still determined to see how close we could get.

The dignitaries started to arrive and it was getting close to showtime. If I was going to make a bold move, now was the time. I saw my former alderman who was now the County Board President and I knew I had to say something. I greeted her and reminded her of who I was and went into my appeal for a ticket. She graciously told me that she didn't have an extra ticket and wished me luck. I kept asking, even some pretty important people that I didn't even know. Everyone looked at me as if they admired my persistence, but couldn't help. I kept asking with a smile believing that somehow ... some way ... we gotta make it in the VIP someway (Shout-out to Jay-Z). Resilience is a mutha and persistence pays off!

The gate ticket agent looked at me like, "Don't even think about it, Sis. It's above me now." I nodded in understanding and kept looking for my next ask. Just as I was about to try to make it back to the section where we were, a man from Pepsico that I'd asked earlier came back out and made a beeline to me excitedly saying, "I got an extra ticket for you!" Then he apologetically said, "But I only have one." I looked at Paul and said, "It's yours buddy. I will watch it from where I can." Paul hesitated, but reached for the ticket before looking at the agent and saying: "How about a 2 for 1 special?" She managed a half smile but said she couldn't. The Pepsico man said, "If they fire you, I'll give you a job." I said, "Wait, I might need a job too. I just left law school to start a business. Can I have your card?" He smiled and obliged my request.

Paul said, "I'm going to wait here with you and see if maybe I can distract the agent and you run into the crowd to blend in." I had to give it to Paul; he was determined and confident that God would position us. I was feeling slightly defeated, but still just grateful to have gotten this far with the lowest general admission ticket that was supposed to place me in front of a screen. I had made it to VIP on a general admission ticket for one of the most coveted historical events of the year (probably the century). I gave Paul a struggle smile and said, "Thank you for your service to the country and for your efforts today. Gon' head in. I'll be all right."

Paul looked me right in the eye and said, "It was great seeing that fire of hope in your eyes. Now it's sad to see you defeated as if you have lost hope before it's over." I felt like he had spoken a whole deep word like he knew my life. It turns out Paul was a Preacher's kid. I said to Paul, "We gave it a few good tries. We've done all we can do and the program is almost starting." He said, "Almost. Let's just wait a few more minutes."

I couldn't do anything but sigh and stay put, but I felt it was a wrap for getting into the gold area. Even still, I thought about what Paul had said and I said just these few words silently to God, "Lord, thank you for bringing me this far. If this is where you want me to be, I accept Your will. Lord, if you see fit for me to be better positioned, please make a way Father. I am grateful for how far you've brought me, but don't believe you've brought me this far to leave me at the door unable to get in." I got chills because I knew that the prayer was about so much more than getting access to that VIP area.

When the Obamas came into term two, I was praying for God to make a way for me to get enough scholarship money to attend a top law school. Now I'd left law school to start a business. It didn't make sense to many, but it did stand to make change for plenty. Right in the midst of me trying to make sense of the deeper meaning, the Cook County Board President came rushing towards the exit holding up a ticket. I saw her and I thought I heard my name, but I didn't want to get my hopes up, as she could have been coming out with a ticket for one of her colleagues with the same name. She was looking at me though! I gave a hopeful grin to which she replied with a head nod before saying, "I got you a ticket Andrea!" I hugged her so quick and strong that I had to apologize. Paul looked up with an "I told you so" grin and said, "See Andrea, you just needed a little faith." He held out his hand and said, "Shall we?"

I walked past the gate agent as if they'd just let me into the VIP side of the best club in town. Even the gate agent had to give me a back pound for my persistence. It didn't really hit me then, but what happened next almost laid me out right there at McCormick Place. As I walked towards the railing, I realized I was in front of the press pit, closer to the stage than any of the major networks. In fact, we were so close that one of my media colleagues gave me his phone to get a closer shot of the stage for him. I couldn't believe this was happening. I tried to take a seat and learned I was actually sitting in the politician's area. Someone mistook me for State's Attorney Kim Foxx. I smiled and told them I was not Foxx, but was such a fan of her inspiring story.

It was time to network before the speech started. As an usher came towards me, I automatically reached for my ticket, ready to let her know that I really was supposed to be there and I had proof that

I did not sneak into this section. Instead of asking me for my stub, she kindly said, "Ma'am, we're about to get started and this section is reserved for the family. "The Family," I said sounding confused and excited at the same time. I said "The Family" again as if she was speaking another language. She smirked and said, "This section is for the President's family." I said, "They my family, Sis!" She laughed and said, "Are you gonna move?" I replied, "Well tell me how close I can get to my Sister/Auntie/Mentor Michelle O." She pointed towards the rail on the end of the first row and said, "Stand there. They'll be coming out in seven minutes and if you're willing to stand the whole time, you'll only have these five seats between you and the first lady."

Let me tell you, I had my flat shoes on and I was ready! I managed to get out, "Thank you" and a tear almost fell as I thought about the favor God had on my life to put me in the best position in some of the most unlikely of places, even when I didn't have the right level of access. God became the ultimate plug and just like that ... access granted!

Valerie Jarrett was sitting at the end of the row with her Mom. One of my fellow fans got too excited and was hovering too closely. Jarrett kindly asked her to give her Mom a little space. The woman looked like she wanted to say something slick, but realized she wasn't sitting on the first row for nothing before she leaned in and asked me, "Sis, who is she?" I wanted to say, "Sis, she is Sis!" Instead, I told her that Jarrett was the Senior Advisor to the

Obama Administration and used to be in an executive leadership role with The Habitat Company. When it comes to law and real estate, I make it my business to know the *Who's Who* and their rise to success, especially if they are Black in business.

I had prepared a 15-second statement, but when THE Michelle Obama came around to shake hands, all I could do was step back and look at her up close. I probably looked like a crazy lady. I'd been taking more pictures of her than of the President, so much so that at one point Mrs. Robinson (the first lady's Mother) looked at me like, "Okay honey, that's enough." The only words that came out were, "OMG, I forgot what I was supposed to say." The tears started to fall and she just stretched her hands out to hug me. I embraced her gently as if she might break, but knowing she wouldn't. I didn't want my excitement to make me hug her too tight. I knew pictures were being taken and I had the ugly cry but I didn't even care. I asked if she would run for office to which she quickly replied, "Oh no, but we still have work to do."

I couldn't even sleep that night. I stayed up screaming sporadically in excitement. One bottle of Love Cork Screw Wine later, I finally went to sleep at 3 am!

First Lady Michelle Obama was overlooked, underestimated, and minimized with the world watching her yet she remained graceful. She really did manage to go high when she really probably wanted to tell some of them to go to hell. She was too poised to say it aloud, but real enough to have thought it. They criticized what she wore and how she looked, but it seemed as if over time she swanned on them. The more they talked, the more pronounced her beauty, impeccable fashion and grace became. She was becoming an iconic first lady, our Forever FLOTUS, and she represented us well because greatness is just truly who we are.

Forever FLOTUS Michelle Obama reminded me of me and what I could become too. Against all odds, I could do what people said I couldn't do. Initially getting admitted to an Ivy League law school was about my perceived ability as a Black girl from the hood. I felt that even if I couldn't afford to attend, the fact that I was admitted somehow affirmed me. It wasn't until later that I realized I didn't need a predominantly white institution with a hefty price tag to tell me I was smart. In fact, I could still be wildly successful without that degree. I was discovering a new way and seeing Michelle Obama live out our ancestors' wildest dreams made me believe that I could go high too, even when they went low. Humble beginnings make for a great testimony when you're determined to work hard and keep the faith.

The little girl inside me smiled.

## Connection Clue

Reflect on a time that God pulled you out of a crowd and had you forego the standard procedure for advancement and preferential treatment not based on your own merit but His favor and grace—a time where you knew without a shadow of a doubt that it was Him.

Once you recall that moment, write down three ways He brought you through and/or helped you be in an even better position after the struggle. What lessons about faith and resilience can you glean from that experience?

You have your own AUDACIOUS story to draw from. If you are compelled to share your story or dive deeper into this topic area, please join us in our Facebook group.

**Audacity Affirmation**

When they start to go extremely low, it is my confirmation that it is time to soar. Eagles don't consort with crows nor play with pigeons. I won't worry about what's on the ground level when it's time to ascend. I will let them go low and continue to hold my head high gracefully.

# Chapter 9

## The Audacity of Saving Grace

While we look not at the things which are seen, but at the things which are not seen: for the things which are seen are temporal; but the things which are not seen are eternal.
2 Corinthians 4:18

I hadn't even told my client what I was going through, how everyone close to me in the "family" I'd known had turned on me, allowing the angriest man I'd known (outside of my father) to use my child to hurt me. I hadn't told her, yet I listened as she told me about her cousin who "was never the same" after her children's father lied and took her children. She hadn't seen them in over two years. My client also shared that the woman had lost her mind, and that although she tried to understand how to fight the system, the judge just kept telling her to be quiet. She left the courtroom forever changed.

I remembered how difficult it is for a mother who doesn't know policy and procedure to represent herself when she doesn't have the money to retain counsel and can't seem to navigate the overwhelmed, and almost always overwhelming, free legal service programs. For a long time, I thought NOT having the knowledge makes it harder to fight. However, I quickly learned that HAVING the knowledge and fighting for basic rights using policy only makes you that much more of a target. I said it before and I'll say it again, when we stand our ground, they try even harder to knock us down to the ground! I listened to her story, and thought about the others I'd heard or seen first-hand.

Instead of anger towards the people who were ignorant enough to try to slander me, I decided to use what God was willing to have me endure for the good of me and the good of many. I felt compassion ... Lord, forgive them for they know not what they do. I'd asked God for the impartation of discernment at the very beginning of my entrepreneurial journey. Throughout the years, from housing struggles, a hospitalization, and nearly losing my sanity when the enemy got too close, God has consistently shown me the true faces of the people around me. It was as if He allowed me to step outside of myself just briefly to see what He was doing, yet not how He was going to do it. Then it got real. He began to unmask everyone around me even as He gave me a clear mirror to see myself in all my glory, flaws, and standing in the full purpose of my own story. God put some Windex on it!

I could see so clearly why He chose me to endure, and why it had to be me to break the chains. For the first time, instead of feeling burdened by the responsibility, I felt honored. It was indeed a privilege despite the pain. I got to be the one God called to shine light in dark places and to champion for justice in a broken system. Of course, it was sometimes heavy despite the blessing attached to it. And I couldn't ignore that it would take faith over fear—and faith by force—to fight such a formidable and oppressive force. Yet I persisted. Admittedly, I didn't have much of a choice; the stakes were too high.

It never felt like much of an honor before, which is part of why I left law school (besides the hiring freezes that meant salaries were less than the debt acquired to get the degree). I simply got tired of fighting. I'd fought the system in criminal court and housing court for myself and on the other side as an intern at the Federal level. I'd seen first-hand how racism pervaded the healthcare system, and the housing and zoning legislation, the two connected by brown fields that minorities inhabited and the EPA nor the FDA could even keep us safe.

Moreover, I never wanted my son to eat flaming hots with Red no. 5 or cheap juice with loads of high fructose corn syrup. That's part of why I started cooking in the shelter because even when you're poor you don't have to eat poorly. That part! When I said this to people around me, the response was as if I was talking bougie Charlie Brown talk. I got much of the same response when I made the decision to homeschool my son. I knew that I needed to learn his unique learning style to best advocate for him in the school setting. I knew I didn't have the support necessary to completely home school, but hearing from Black families that had successfully homeschooled their children and the benefits of doing so convinced me to ignore the naysayers and do what was best for my son.

When he did return to the school system, the transition was rough for more reasons than one. The schools expect you to just drop off your child at the door and go about your way. I started a routine of walking him to his locker, and getting his day started with the same positive affirmation every day: "I am strong. I am powerful. I am capable. I am smart. I can do anything I put my mind to. My Mommy and Daddy love me and Jesus does too. Today will be a great day. I am going to make it a great day!"

After the first couple of weeks, administrators told me that I couldn't walk my son to the lockers and needed to drop him off at the door instead. I knew there was a difference between how children from two-parent wealthy homes were treated and the treatment my son and I received. Furthermore, it amazed me that when I started to volunteer with the organization that got me a scholarship to attend private school, I was able to see first-hand how differently schools up north in more affluent communities were run with parental engagement at the core.

My son had a habit of running off to the playground, while staff told his classmates to line up along the wall at pickup. One day I went to the office after looking for him for nearly 20 minutes and asked if he could be paged on the intercom. I looked for him for 30 minutes before asking staff and security to assist me. They begrudgingly did. We found him shortly after. It was over an hour after pickup time. When I found him, I was relieved and in a rush to make it to work, since I was already running late. I was zipping his coat when the lady said, "Can you sign him out?" I was confused. The sign-out book was for late pickups. She knew that I'd been there on time and had looked for my son for over an hour with staff who could not account for his whereabouts. Despite this, she insisted that I sign the late pick-up log. I asked, "Should I sign the time I got here or the time we found him?" She said, "You can put the time that it is right now." I knew right then that they knew that this could potentially be seen as negligence and were making an initial attempt to shift blame just in case I sent another email shedding light on things they wished to keep under wraps.

I left the school feeling so tired of having to fight for even the basic of rights. Trying to enforce the policy was a job in and of itself. I mean, who do you even call when racism rears its ugly head? Are the colleagues working for the same system that the perpetrators represent expected to hold each other accountable? As we walked to the bus stop, I saw a Maserati pull up to pick up kids from the after school program that I couldn't afford so my son couldn't stay. I thought to myself, "It's cool. If I just make enough money in this business, I can move to a good neighborhood and he won't have to attend school through a Federal program for displaced children.

Once we are not poor anymore, they won't treat us poorly anymore." Even as I thought that, I knew deep down that even having money couldn't protect us from the hatred.

Weeks later, I was coming from downtown and a train malfunction had the train stopped on the tracks for nearly 30 minutes. I'd called the school nearly 20 times with no answer. When I finally connected to the bus to drop me off two blocks away from the school, it was over an hour after school let out. My phone had died just as I got off the bus and here I was at the door ringing the bell, nearly out of breath. The principal, a white woman and Harvard graduate, always acted very apprehensive around me, almost like she was terrified of me, even when I attempted to be kind and cordial with her. I was firm, but being firm as a Black woman easily gets you labeled as an angry Black woman.

I stood outside the school ringing the doorbell for a couple minutes before the principal answered with, "How can I help you?" I said, "I am here for my son. I've been calling the school for over an hour." She could see and hear me through the video intercom. She told me that she thought that he was picked up. I said, "I can't confirm that and my phone battery is dead." It was freezing outside and that woman continued to talk to me through an intercom. She went on to say that she "thinks" his tutor picked him up, but no one signed him out late that day. I said sternly but respectfully, "Ma'am, as you can see, this is Jeremiah's mother. Today is not tutoring pick up. I am telling you that I cannot confirm that my son has been picked up and you are telling me you 'think' that he was picked up which isn't very comforting." She responded in a way that reminded me that you have to be docile when disagreeing or attempting to ask for basic cooperation. She said, "I'm not going to help you if you're going to speak to me like that." I asked if she could call my Grandmother to confirm and she came back to tell me that she also didn't have my son. I asked again if she could call the police, to which she finally agreed.

As I started to call out my son's name, I saw someone walking towards an open side door. I was able to run in before the door slammed. The woman said, "Can I help you?" Nearly out of breath, I said, "I am Aric Jeremiah's Mom" to which she replied, "Yeah, I heard about you. Just wait here because the building is closed and the principal said you are not to come in." Before I could say anything, my son came banging on the glass. She let him in and he started crying. I said, "Jeremiah, where were you?" He said, "I was playing and then the last kid was picked up and no one answered the door so I was under the sliding board of the playground." I felt so defeated. The woman didn't even say a word. She simply held the door open like, "Okay, you got your baby. Now get out."

I couldn't believe it. I just couldn't see how it got so bad that a seven-year-old could be left on the playground in the winter for hours and no one even cared enough to say, "Come sit down inside for a moment." They surely hated me, but I didn't know that hatred would adversely impact how they cared for my child. I'd already had the police called on me three times at that point and I was so enraged that I knew if they called this time it would be for a reason. I cried silent tears on the way to the bus stop holding my son's hand that was as cold as an icicle. I felt helpless, but I felt that if I made noise now about this somebody would listen.

I contacted the Office of the Inspector General of the Chicago Public Schools the next day and started the process of submitting a formal complaint. The legal department called me the next day requesting a statement. I called three different attorneys and the process to even get them to take the case was cumbersome to say the least. I got referred to others who specialized in educational law and one that wanted me to pay a couple thousand to take on the case. I went to a PTA meeting with seven people and a camera crew talking about how my son was left on the playground in the cold. I was met with more disregard. Only one woman afterwards gave me her email address saying that she wanted to help. I wondered how differently this case would've went if we'd been one of the wealthy families that already had a lawyer on retainer.

I felt so disempowered and the nonchalant response I got led me to believe that no one was appalled about my Black son being left on a playground in the cold. I had family members selling snow cones in front of the same school I was trying to sue telling me to "just let it go and move on." It's like we never know how to fight against the system and even if we know how they wear us down by dragging it out and making it expensive to fight back. I was poor and despite knowing that I'd been wronged and that the school was liable, I didn't even have the means to fight back even with evidence and support.

My son was left on the playground for hours in nearly freezing temperature weather and they didn't even want to have a formal meeting about it. I went to the school multiple times requesting a meeting after several emails went unanswered, only to have the police called on me. When they arrived, they'd tell administration that all they could do was walk me out of the building since my only offense was requesting a meeting. After several emails, I received a response that the school officials would meet with me but only if I agreed to meet with them alone. In essence, they were preventing me from recording the meeting and making it so that I couldn't have any witnesses. They were playing legal hardball and I didn't even have the means to play ball. I asked, "Would you tell a two-parent household that only one parent could come?" As a single mother, I felt that I deserved to have at least one witness to any communication with the school.

One thing I found to be peculiar is that the principal never spoke to me about my concerns, not any of them, not even once. Instead she sent the assistant principal, a Black woman, to deal with me.

This was the same woman that called the police on me the very first day I came in to register my son, simply because I had conflicting information on what the policy was for children who didn't live in the neighborhood. I'm mentioning the policy here so anyone in that position will understand that schools have the discretion of registering students before or on the first day when they are in the STLS program. The problem is that often discretion breeds discrimination. I won't go too deep into all of that here, but the bottom line is that schools tend to register as many non-STLS students as possible so they'll have to include fewer STLS students.

Another policy surrounds field trips. The first field trip came around and I paid the $15 dollar fee for my son to attend. Shortly after, I learned that per STLS policy, families enrolled in the school through this program are not required to pay for field trips. I notified them of the policy and begrudgingly they refunded the money, but that seemed to mark the second start of things becoming immensely difficult for me at the school.

I soon learned that the assistant principal hated me with every fiber of her being and sought to make it difficult for me every chance she could. One particular day, I was there again requesting a meeting and she'd had it with me recording and emailing and just went off. She told administration to call the police because "she was sick of my crazy ass coming there being demanding." She went on to say, "You better get your 'Go Fund Me' ass out of my building." I had raised some money online to attend law school and apparently she had done her homework. I'd seen her kind before, mean older Black women who seemed to dislike younger women unless they were sucking up to them. It was interesting that the white principal sent her to deal with me and she did so in the most dishonorable and disrespectful way. Often they send us to deal with us on some COINTELPRO. Why is it such a challenge for some of us to just show basic respect for one another at times?

I went live on social media about the ordeal in front of the school and another Black parent stopped and told me that she too had the police called on her and knew a couple of other Black parents who also had the police called on them. Before I knew it, I had parents inboxing me from Ray Elementary and other schools where they had similar challenges advocating for their kids. I didn't have all the answers, but I knew I wasn't alone in the struggle and united we are so much stronger. I was more united with other parents than my own people. But life has been my courtroom, my trial, my acquittal and my dismissal.

Within the first few months of my son's enrollment, the assistant principal challenged whether I was actually displaced and prompted an investigation as to my qualification for the Student in Temporary Living Situations (STLS) stating that I didn't "appear to be homeless." It's sad that you're not entitled to even your integrity in the midst of overcoming when people in high positions abuse their power. I didn't fit the stereotype and I didn't walk lightly either. Perhaps, I wasn't "humble" enough. What does humble mean exactly ... walking with my head down? What saddened me most is that I actually expected it from the white principal who permeated Harvard elitism, but I didn't expect it from a Black woman. I am all for the sisterhood, but some of the women who could be more caring towards young mothers seem to despise us more than build us up. I guess just because you're a sista doesn't make you my sister. You can be an enemy too, and perhaps the worst enemy.

Interestingly, during the pandemic the assistant principal became the principal of the school. An article published in the *Hyde Park Herald* quoted her as saying that her inspiration to become a principal was the power that the principal had when she was a child attending another school in elitist Hyde Park. It was the power that she loved, not the position and not the people—well at least not the people that fit outside the narrow box of what she deemed befitting of respect. Again, never let the enemy or people who despise you be responsible for educating your child. I said that twice because it's that's important.

It took me discussing the issue with a colleague for her to tell me something I hadn't previously realized. She said, "Andrea, wealthy families have a family table. In addition to two or three types of attorneys on retainer, there should also be an accountant, a tax consultant and an insurance professional. When an issue arises, you shouldn't have to figure out what to do or how to move. You pay people to advise you and handle the matter." It seemed like a far reach, but the more and more I scaled, the more I realized the critical need for protecting your assets and having the means to defend yourself **when** an injustice arises.

A Facebook friend, Whit Devereaux, shared an incredible Scripture Isaiah 54:11-17 that truly encapsulates the nature of the fight involved when dealing with the legal system. This is *The Message* version. Although it's long, it's so powerful that I had to include it.

"Afflicted city, storm-battered, unpitied:

I'm about to rebuild you with stones of turquoise,

Lay your foundations with sapphires,

construct your towers with rubies,

Your gates with jewels,

and all your walls with precious stones.

All your children will have God for their teacher—

what a mentor for your children!

You'll be built solid, grounded in righteousness,

far from any trouble—nothing to fear!

far from terror—it won't even come close!

If anyone attacks you,
don't for a moment suppose that I sent them,
And if any should attack,
nothing will come of it.
I create the blacksmith
who fires up his forge
and makes a weapon designed to kill.
I also create the destroyer—
but no weapon that can hurt you has ever been forged.
Any accuser who takes you to court
will be dismissed as a liar.
This is what God's servants can expect.
I'll see to it that everything works out for the best."

## Connection Clue

Wickedness in high places is difficult to fight against, yet there are some of us equipped and called to the task of eradicating bias, dispelling myths and educating people to do the same when they face similar situations.

What battle are you avoiding because of its difficulty? How are you educating yourself on the preparation required to fight the good fight with grace and effectiveness?

You're not ranting and you are not alone. You may need to reposition your message and speak to the right people in decision-making positions.

**Audacity Affirmation**

I am equipped to fight against injustice because I survived the things they used to try to break me. My voice and the courage to speak out properly equips me because as Dr. Martin Luther King, Jr. reminded us "an injustice anywhere is a threat to justice everywhere." We have to be willing to get into good trouble in order to fight the good and very necessary fight for fairness and equality. I run with the strength that my ancestors walked with!

# Chapter 10

## Concluding Thoughts: The Next Phase

And be not conformed to this world: but be ye transformed by the renewing of your mind, that ye may prove what is that good, and acceptable, and perfect, will of God.
Romans 12:2

Audacity is defined in the dictionary as a willingness to take bold risks. I'll add to that definition having the bravery to do something that could offend others or upset the enemy's plans. *The Audacity of Overcoming* is the resiliency spirit of the underdog against formidable obstacles. There is a particular persistence, a brazen boldness, and an unrelenting force. It is a full faith walk rooted in certainty and blessed assurance. It is also a costly confirmation that hope will bring you out that much better.

**There is an art to pressing forward and doing so with such grace that your ability to withstand becomes a blueprint of overcoming to inspire others to also grow and glow through gracefully. The pressure process births a diamond. The crushing of the olive produces the oil. But yes, the oil costs; your pain is the purchase price. Pay your dues; learn the lessons and expect the blessing.**

The oil will protect your anointing and lead to your reward. Remember the eucalyptus seed has to germinate after literally being under fire. Often there is a forcing that takes place to push and catapult us. It is uncomfortable. It is stretching. I've been realigned, repositioned, reassigned and rearranged, but I've also been restored amidst chaos, confusion and turmoil. God can use it all. Not a hurricane, a crisis, depression, nor an intermittent pandemic can counter God's plan. Even those adversities can be used for His perfect purpose. Willingly accept His will, leaning not to your own understanding, but fully trusting that He sees your struggle and knows your midnight cry.

I remember when I was going through postpartum depression. I couldn't quite figure out who the new me was. But I knew my life was forever changed. I didn't mourn the old version, but didn't quite understand how to embrace the new one. I truly believe that my son's love saved me in my darkest moments. The love between a mother and son is the closest earthly reflection of God's love that I can fathom. I remember crying many nights while my son laid on my arm cuddled under me in bed. One night, he woke up while I was crying and put his hand on my face. He wasn't even nine months yet. He had a look of concern on his face as he knew I was hurting. He gently rested his little face on my cheek and every so often he'd pop his face up and look at me. I looked back saying, "Let's go back to sleep son," reassuring him that I was okay.

He had his own room, his own full-sized bed, and a vintage bassinet, but he would still cry if he didn't sleep with me. People would say you're gonna spoil that baby, but the truth was I felt just as much comfort knowing he was right there because the room right next door seemed too far away. I overcame being a single mother and when it got tough, I toughened up, yet I also knew when it was time to sit down and rest my cape.

In what areas do you need to slow down and how can you use your connections in other areas where you need to act expeditiously?

You can't change the world and your circumstances without the one that formed the world and made you. Stay connected, especially in a storm. God is a guide, a resource, a surge protector and gives you elevator lift!

**"One shot to your heart without breaking yo' skin, no one has the power to hurt you like your kin. Kept it inside, didn't tell no one else. Didn't even want to admit it to yourself."**

**—Indie Arie, "Get It Together"**

When the backbone of the family is the breakdown of the community and the downfall of the people, God will still make a way for a messenger to prevail. That is why the black sheep is typically the one to break generational curses. The love of God will cause you to forgive people who were responsible for your setbacks. God can use even the weapons of the enemy to advance you for His agenda.

The struggle is necessary to resurrect the blueprint to not only survive but to also thrive. Be done with the poverty mindset. Absorb your character for greatness even amidst confusion and chaos. In all thy getting, get an understanding. Once you have that ultimate understanding, you are forever changed for there's no way that knowing what you know now, you can remain the same.

In a race, you often can't see where the runner ahead of you is going. You can only see so far after the baton is passed. Don't seek approval from disapproving faces. Maybe it's not that they don't believe in you. It could be that they were never brave enough to believe in themselves to go after their dreams so their apprehension about you taking on the risk to dream a big dream scares them. Nevertheless, you have to soar fearlessly, without the weight of their words and you absolutely cannot afford to let their doubt dim your light.

## Ground Transportation

Sometimes we want to fly, but we only have the funds for Greyhound. Sometimes we don't appreciate that even though flying gets us there faster, at least we are moving on the Greyhound. The key though is to use that extra time wisely. If you have a 40-hour train trip, you could have written most of a book. Reputedly, John Boyne wrote

*The Boy in the Striped Pajamas* in two and a half days.

## Takeoff: I See the Victory

The proper weight to take off requires a release. The pressure produces the elements for lift. The lift is required to truly soar. Sometimes you're at the bus station waiting for a delayed bus when your calling requires you to be at the airport for an on-time departure!

## Get in the Proper Position!

The port is a conduit, a place where people go to seek refuge in the storm. My prayer is that this book is a port for people seeking refuge and restoration, a manual for overcoming adversity and not just surviving it but growing through it. It is a guide for actually achieving what would have been impossible had you not gone through the required critical phases.

The pain of the critical phase is a necessary part of the flight that will catapult you to your next level. A lot of times people will ask the question, "Why do I have to struggle through this if I'm so destined?" That's the answer because you are destined. Even your struggle will birth your success. There is significance in your struggle. There is a resolve at the other side of your resilience. There is a reason; the struggle is temporary in a certain season. God prepares a seat for you in the presence of your enemies.

## Unexpected Turbulence

Don't lose focus or get nervous when you hear the PSA warning you of unexpected turbulence. Don't turn around no matter what anyone says. If you knew how close you were, you would put on earbuds and tune in completely to what He is saying to you.

Every adversity that you went through lines up so perfectly that you knew He was doing it for you all along and that He had your overcoming in mind. He did it for you! You can't even reconcile how to tell somebody what He did and just how awesome and amazing it was. God gave me something to grow with and something to sow with. What He has for me is so much more than my plan could ever be.

While attending the Rolling Out Ride Conference, who are you rolling out with? Who are you riding with?

You cannot take everyone on the journey with you. You cannot mistake a friend for an enemy. There's too much riding on your success.

## Connecting Flights

The road to success and your life destiny is very often not linear. It is full of delays, re-routes and both scheduled and unscheduled stops. Connections are good, but God is navigating the connections. It is His plans unfolding that is sending the help. I give Him the honor while thanking the people that He sent.

There a lot of things, people, organizations, memberships and circles you can be connected to, but the best connection you can ever have is with your Creator. There will be times when the people you've known for decades, or maybe even since birth, won't understand you. To be honest, they may start to seem and sound strange to you too. Don't become so distracted in the layover season that you miss your connection flight.

Who is powerful enough to prolong your struggle and sabotage your success? You cannot afford to risk it all for someone who is prone to risk and consumed with consistency of problems, yet offers few solutions. Get around people who are positioned to help you excel in a powerful way. They will not always be people you expected. In fact, it may be people you least expected to have anything to even bless you with, but when God chooses to bless you in a way that only He can, things align in a powerful way. Then you have to walk boldly and embody the light when you move through dark spaces.

## Baggage Claim and Extra Baggage

You're almost there! Then you go to a carousel to claim your baggage. Hopefully, you pack more strategically than I used to so that you don't overpack. However, if you are like me, you may tend to carry the weight of things you hold on to unnecessarily on the journey. What extra baggage are you carrying?

What role did you play in adverse situations? I think we often process best by moving on past the hurt and unburdening ourselves of all that extra weight. Better still, let me carry on instead and check this baggage.

## Landing the Plane

God has the perfect purpose in everything! The egg met the sperm at the ideal time to create you. The Ultimate Plug plugged you to win the race, but you have to stay connected to get an energy supply. There are people running around looking for a lil' juice. Different chargers charge your phone at different speeds. Make sure you're connected to The Source because God Is The Ultimate Plug to give you The Audacity of Overcoming!

I've known rivers. I've known struggles. Each and every one was purposed and none of it was in vain. It was all orchestrated and connected, in every small detail. I went to undergraduate school on a former plantation and law school in a former sundown town in a city nicknamed "Lake No Negro."

But everywhere I am, and everywhere I will be, I will always be Nikki from the southside of Chicago.

**Here's to my first bestselling book and more after this one. Now, that's some audacity!**

## JOURNEY NOTES

- Check your passenger travel list.
- The critical phases of flight are takeoff and landing.
- Descent comes before final approach.
- In the unlikely event of an emergency, secure yourself first.

# About the Author

Andrea is an ambitious mother, business owner, native Chicagoan, and philanthropist who diligently works to build a legacy brand to secure her son's future while creating and supporting initiatives that contribute to domestic violence prevention, senior story sharing, as well as economic and youth empowerment. Her current outreach includes fundraising scholarships for students attending HBCUs through the Audacious Midwest To South Scholarship / EBJV Memorial Foundation.

Through Live In The Content Kitchen™, Andrea candidly interviews professionals and everyday extraordinary people over conversations, cocktails and cuisine. When she isn't speaking or working, she enjoys cooking, traveling, and creating new opportunities and adventures for clients and colleagues. Andrea is primarily based in Chicago, but enjoys taking her talents cross-country and is looking forward to taking *The Audacity of Overcoming* international.

Follow Andrea's Audacious Adventures by connecting with the GITUP Movement online.

**www.theaudacityofovercoming.com**

**IG: @AndreaIsThePlug**

**TikTok: @AndreaIsThePlug**

**FB: bit.ly/GITUPOnFacebook**

# Acknowledgements

## To My Sisters

Listen more than you speak so you learn and observe from hearing and implementation. Operate with peace, understanding, discernment and wisdom in who you are.

Seek to understand, and at the point which you overstand things, speak truth to power and be the light, especially when you know you're in the right. Stand firm. Use your voice boldly, especially when it shakes. Hold your head up high even if you let them see a tear run down your face. Be your best self; there is nobody like you. You should only strive to be you, your best you, while learning to fall more in love with you every day. Laying down the fight to embrace people and doing everything in love will always prevail in adverse situations.

## Fallen Guides & Resting Angels RIP

Lynndyal W. Arnold

Wesley D. Houseton

Clinton Thompson

Bishop Arthur M. Brazier

Robert Gordon

Mark S. Allen

Ms. Pearline Wiley

Ms. Lois Outlaw

Cassandra Campbell

Chavanna Prather

Aina Horne

Devon Wiley

Henry Wright

Nikki Ford

# Ways To Be Audacious

## Contribute to:

**Audacious Midwest To South Scholarship /
EBJV Memorial Foundation**

For in-kind support or matching donation pledges, please email us at connect@theaudacityofovercoming.com.

## Purchase Audacious Merchandise

**The INBox**

A custom-curated theme with each box release, once per quarter.

Shop on the website for the custom box and other branded apparel: www.theaudacityofovercoming.com.

# Resources & Connections Guide: Pass the Plug

**For continued resources and membership opportunities for exclusive offerings, join the GITUP FB community at: bit.ly/GITUPOnFacebook.**

*There will be podcast announcements and exclusive interviews with audacious leaders in mental health, business and youth empowerment arenas.*

*We will be interviewing mindset coaches, singers, beauty professionals and other amazing global-minded power brokers.*

## Sharing Your Story

***Publishing Your Story***

Renée Purdie, Bodacious Book Birther
Email: info@msrisingstar.com

***Marketing Your Brand Story***

Andrea M. Thompson, Courageous Content Creator
Email: connect@theaudacityofovercoming.com

## Personal/Professional Development

***Dr. Jeanne Porter King***

www.jeanneporterking.com

## Health and Wellness

***Follow Live In The Content Kitchen™ Facebook page!***

https://www.facebook.com/ContentInTheKitchen

*Get a taste for this foodie's movement by visiting the recipes in the back of this book.*

**Quarterly custom-curated beauty and relaxation events**

# Discussion Questions

1. What does audacity mean to you? Share your answers in our Facebook group or tag us on social media with #TheAudacityofOvercoming. Include a selfie with your copy of the book and be placed in a competition to receive The Audacity of Overcoming (TAoO) merchandise!

2. How would you describe "The Audacity of Overcoming" (not the book, but we welcome a review), but for this question we mean what does it mean and look like? What are the characteristics of "The Audacity of Overcoming"?

3. Does Michelle Obama's famous quote "When They Go Low, We Go High" sometimes make you feel that taking the high road can allow undeserving people to get the best of you as we are told to turn the other cheek?

4. How do we balance the aforementioned with knowing that vengeance belongs to the Lord, while also balancing holding ourselves and others accountable?

5. What are some takeaways on the importance of healthy daddy/daughter/mommy/son relationships? What are some key things that are important for fathers and mothers to know?

6. What are four core values/characteristics that contribute to being relentless and resilient in the pursuit of greatness and success?

7. What things did you perceive to be flaws in your younger years that you now see as perfect imperfections that you are now able to embrace as unique parts of yourself?

8. Parenting: Being a Single mother and trying to co-parent can be challenging, yet very rewarding. Co-parenting can further complicate healthy parenting. What are some of the key things that you have observed or implemented and have found to be useful and effective in instilling values in children, even when the parents are raising the children separately? What is some solid advice that you have found to be useful, particularly when it comes to raising Black young men?

9. Reflect on a time when you had to forgive someone who inflicted a great deal of heartache, shame and hurt. In hindsight, how did forgiving (in spite of whether or not they deserved it) help you to get free?

10. Injustice and discrimination are sometimes the most difficult atrocities to battle. The devastation of bias chips away at your soul. Many of us have witnessed firsthand or via societal exposure death and disappointment at the hands of people and systems sworn in and in position to serve and protect. How has the trauma of bias, discrimination, and injustice affected you and/or those you love? What have been some positive steps towards healing that you have found to be effective?

## Bonus Questions

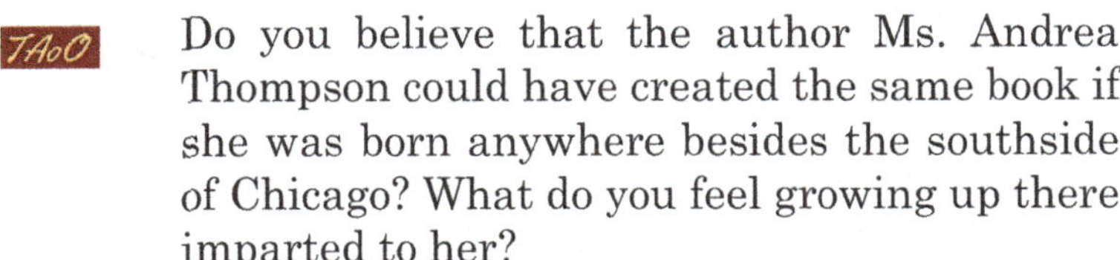

TAoO Do you believe that the author Ms. Andrea Thompson could have created the same book if she was born anywhere besides the southside of Chicago? What do you feel growing up there imparted to her?

TAoO What are the biggest takeaways you have from reading *The Audacity of Overcoming*?

# Live in the Content Kitchen™ Audacious Recipes

*As mentioned in "90 Days Homeless," food brings everybody to the table and fosters community and familial ties. We have so much in store for Live In The Content Kitchen™. In the meantime, here's a taste.*

## Southern A-Town Peach Cobbler

*Atlanta is known for peaches, but in my heart Arkansas is known for peach cobbler! Here's a quick version, similar to the one I made in South Africa!*

*Total Cooking Time: 45 minutes to an hour*

**Ingredients:**

- Pillsbury Dough (I like to use name brand if I don't have time for Andrea's brand–Granny's dough made from scratch. The Live in the Content Kitchen™ Cookbook will have the dough from scratch version.)
- Canned Del Monte Peaches (I know people use fresh peaches, but I usually do fresh blackberries for that kind of cobbler, but canned for peach cobbler.)
- Domino Sugar (the Domino brand is really important for some reason. However, use the brown sugar version though I was trained on the white sugar recipe.)
- McCormick Nutmeg (I did make it with fresh nutmeg that I ground while in Portland and it was pretty tasty.)
- Butter (It's extremely important, perhaps more than anything else, that you do not use margarine, and please use premium butter.)

**Method:**

1. Roll out the dough and cut it into 3-inch strips.
2. Here's where you butter the bottom of the pan and begin the layering process. I typically start with fruit keeping some of the syrup from the can because a dry peach cobbler is not a good peach cobbler! On the other hand, if you keep too much of the syrup, the sugar makes water too so then you'll have peach cobbler soup! Alternatively, I have seen some people start with an unsliced crust bottom but that may originate from another southern state.
3. After a nice layer of peaches distributed evenly, add in sprinkles of nutmeg. I can't say how much 'cause Granny didn't measure, but I know if you use too much the syrup will be too brown and your nutmeg will overpower the dish. The ancestors will drop an intuition in your shondo if you play "Come On In The Room" by the Georgia Mass Choir while you prepare it.
4. Cut medium slices of butter on top of the layer of nutmeg covered peaches.
5. Pour about a half cup of sugar over it before proceeding with your first layer of crust slices across.
6. Repeat the layering.
7. For the top layer you want to be sure to interlock the strips of crust to make a visually appealing display. Brush butter over the crust strips to give it a nice golden look. Sprinkle a teaspoon of sugar over the top of the crust.
8. Cover top with aluminum foil and place in a preheated oven on 350 degrees. (Make sure it's Fahrenheit and not Celsius so you don't have a slightly burned peach cobbler like I did the first time

I made it in South Africa.) About 25 minutes in, you can remove the aluminum foil.

*The peach cobbler came from Granny and in honor of my late Paw Paw, The Singing Ice Cream Man (an Arkansas native like Granny), I've selected these delicious Kilwins frozen treats to complement this Southern Sweet:*

- New Orleans Praline Pecan
- Maple Walnut
- Sea Salt Caramel

*Shout out to owners, mother/daughter duo, Jacqueline and Janel Jackson with two Kilwins locations downtown, one on Michigan Avenue and one at Navy Pier, and the original location in Hyde Park's Harper Court. Keep these locations in mind for your next Chicago sweet adventure!*

***Beverage Pair Recommendation****: The Audaci-Tea®, a strong and lightly sweet flavored black tea with a hint of brown sugar*

## Sautéed Pear & Apple Gâteau

*Total Cooking Time: You shall notice a golden-brown crispness and the ancestors shall notify you of its completion.*

**Ingredients:**

- 3 Granny Smith apples
- 2 pears

*There are literally thousands, actually over 2,000, types of pears! Who would have thought it? Anjou or Bartlett are recommended. Surprisingly the ripest one ... the one that looks like it's no longer useful ... serves best in this recipe. Yes, He will use what you thought to discard as no longer in season. Ayyyee Shondo! Sometimes you get a word while you cook, and even more so often while you eat (like in the 90 Days Homeless Chapter.)*

*Okay, back to the recipe just in case you're at the store like, "Okay, just tell me if it's the red, green or brown pear?!" Grab the brown.*

- ~1 Tablespoon cinnamon
- ~ ½ teaspoon nutmeg (very little!)
- 1 Tablespoon Vanilla extract
- ~½ cup of brown sugar, a little more or perhaps a half a teaspoon of agave or raw honey as a substitute for less brown sugar
- 1–2 Tablespoon butter
- ¼ cup of caramel-flavored coffee creamer. (If you choose, go ahead and have the audacity to use your favorite milk substitute or alternate flavor because well, "That's yo' Business!" Shout out to Tabitha Brown.)

**Method:**

1. Cut the apples and pears into medium thin slices.
2. Squeeze fresh lemon juice on the apples.
3. Slightly season apple pear mix before placing in skillet. Season just a lil' bit more during the cooking process.
4. Let settle and sizzle, turning the mix every so often until sugar caramelizes giving you a glaze that will soften the apples when you cover the skillet and reduce the heat. (This glaze can be poured over pancakes or waffles for a breakfast treat. Live In The Content Kitchen™ recommends Michelle's Syrup.)

*If you're looking for a dessert after dinner, pour the glaze over a slice of pound cake or caramel cake. Live In The Content Kitchen™ recommends Brown Sugar Bakery in Chicago. They ship too! Shout out to Stephanie Hart who I call the heart of baking. She's had several notable icons visiting, including Vice President Kamala Harris.*

**Pairs Well With:**

*Love Cork Screw*
*"Touch The Sky"*

Made in the USA
Monee, IL
13 February 2023